Cherry Farcical

A Ridiculously Unrealistic Attempt at Resurrecting American Literary Humor

(You with the clown shoes and orange hair. Move on. There's nothing here for you.)

Doug Miller

ISBN-13: 978-1515298892

DEDICATION

A mention of Mark is required. I think he may well be the only person who unequivocally encourages me to continue producing what you're about to encounter. It's what you'd expect from a life-long friend...

TABLE OF CONTENTS

KNOTS TO YOU

A former teacher is suing the Cincinnati school district, saying she was discriminated against because of her rare phobia: a fear of young children. [The woman] said that when she was transferred to the district's middle school, the children set off her phobia, causing her blood pressure to soar and forcing her to retire. [She] said her phobia falls under the federal American with Disabilities Act, and the transfer violated the law.

– Associated Press

Yes, your honor. It's been made clear to me that this deposition is being recorded for use by the U.S. Attorney's Office, and that everything I say can and will be held against me.

Legally, that is. You understand, of course, that if I were forced to come into actual physical contact with my testimony, a rare and oftentimes comical skin disorder most likely would cause my eyebrows to phosphoresce. In fact, if you don't mind, it might be better if you positioned the microphone a little farther from my face. You won't be able to understand a thing if my tongue swells.

My name is Dominic Shortshaft, plaintiff in Phobic Man v. Helmschmidt Haberdashery, and the facts of my circumstance are these:

In 1997, the men's clothing emporium where I worked – once owned and operated by my father – fell by gambling debt into the hands of Mortimer Helmschmidt, an uncle on my mother's side. Normally, Morty's three-of-a-kind would not have stood to dad's straight flush, but just at the wrong moment the pull-chain snapped and the toilet failed to operate, giving my uncle a chance to retrieve his cards. They were wet, but undeniable winners.

I was kept on, due in large part to what Morty described as my – quote – "unique ability to transform a routine inseam measurement into a strangely satisfying experience" – unquote. That, and the fact that nobody on the entire Eastern Seaboard understands the intricacies of argyle sock thread count better than yours truly. I mean, I don't want to brag or anything, but when it comes to plaid stockings, I'm always a step ahead. It's a gift.

Encouraged by progressive labor practices – when Chinese take-out arrived with too few utensils, for instance, the owner generously permitted the use of shoehorns – I began to enjoy a measure of success. In fact, what previously might have been described as a window box of clients blossomed into a small garden, watered by my reputation as an attendant who could pleat pants with his teeth. In the parlance of the business, things were unfolding remarkably well... until the necktie imperative.

Of course, your honor. I'd be glad to elaborate. Ever since ninth-grade gym class, when a misunderstanding about how to properly step into a jock strap led to a near fatal constriction of my airway, I have suffered from an unnatural fear of any article of clothing that looks like it has even the remotest chance of interfering with my respiratory function.

Difficult to fathom, perhaps, but true nonetheless. I once was hospitalized when, during an especially overzealous hug, I became entangled in my Great Aunt Yetta's bra strap – a trauma that eventually required extraction with the Jaws of Life.

Despite my affliction, I managed to secure a position in the men's clothing business by relying on a series of unlikely feints and avoidances. When it came time for a customer to choose a necktie, for example, I suddenly would be "called" to a dressing room to assist with a client intent on blaming a size misprint for his inability to condense 300 pounds into a pair of 34-waist gabardines. Once, at my lowest point, I ran to the other end of the store and pretended to be a mannequin. Fully aware of my ruse, the customer forced me to stand motionless while he was meticulously fitted for two more suits.

Over time I was able to adapt, moderating my fear by learning to fashion a passable half-Windsor – a knot I could execute while holding my breath. I managed to get by until 2003, when Morty suddenly decreed that continued employment would hinge on my capacity to master the dreaded full-Windsor.

Ignoring my impassioned plea for mercy – and knowing full well that the new policy could cost me my life – he remained adamant in his demand, bringing my career to an ignominious end and forcing me into early retirement. Thus, I find myself here, defending my subsequent claim of discrimination under the federal Americans With Disabilities Act.

So that's my story, your honor. Are there any further questions? I see. In that case, I wonder if I might be permitted to leave. Late for an appointment? Well, no, but I would like an opportunity to floss before I start my new job. I beg your pardon? Why, no. I don't mind telling you. I have nothing to hide.

I work in the Men's Department at Macy's... pleating pants.

MAKING THE BED WON'T NECESSARILY LAND YOU IN IT

When the news came across CNN, I was unloading the dishwasher and folding my underwear. Wait a minute. Now I'm not so sure. I could have been folding the dishwasher and unloading my underwear, but that sounds a little brazen even for me. Damn. This new study has me so unnerved, it's entirely possible I was washing my wares under a dish.

The point is, I was doing what comes naturally to every red-blooded, fair-minded male who's managed to read *The Feminine Mystique* a page and a half at a time while "mistakenly" flipping through the wrong book in the Women and Sexuality aisle at Barnes & Noble. I was rejecting the callous idea, apparently monumentalized by earlier generations of American men, that grocery shopping, cleaning, cooking and breast-feeding are tasks traditionally relegated to the lady of the house.

No, that's not a misprint. I said breast-feeding. There's an odd-looking piece of paraphernalia you can clamp on for the purpose of sharing even that womanly task – although I'd highly recommend disengaging from it before wandering through a revolving door.

I imagine myself, after all, to be a liberated male – instructed in the ways of gender equality and, in the interest of marital bliss, more than willing to pull my own weight. That, by the way, is becoming increasingly difficult due to an unholy affinity for artisanal breads and red zinfandels – a bit of personal shame I ante up in hopes of convincing the jury that the cards I hold carry the uncorrupted trump power of pure egalitarianism. Setting myself up to be the grantee of appreciative sexual favors has nothing at all to do with it. OK. Maybe it has a little to do with it.

Oh, who am I kidding. I put my own laundry through the hot-cold cycle just to generate a little extra steam. That's why my shorts are all in a knot over a recent study in the *American Sociological Review*. It turns out that married men who deliberately spend time washing the dishes and checking sell-by dates in the produce section at Stop & Shop® report having less frequent sex than husbands who stick to more traditionally masculine jobs like home repairs and taking out the garbage.

Stunned, I delved deeper into a *HealthDay* article reporting on the blasphemous research. When it comes to chores, it claimed, equality between the sexes doesn't necessarily lead to a turned-on spouse. Determined to drain what little air remained in my more-labor-means-more-loving balloon, it went on to cite the study author, who unabashedly declared that "While wives tend to be more satisfied with the marriage (when there aren't issues about housework), it doesn't translate to sex if the man helps."

The upshot? Even though a wife says she likes having her husband help around the house, his well-intentioned efforts may end up turning him into more of a helpmate and less of an object of desire.

Great. That's just what I need: to become less of an object of desire than I already am. I mean, even now, in my shining egalitarian armor, there's a damn good chance that on any given day I'll lose to the seductive allure of a simmering pot roast or *Dancing With the Stars*.

Well, that's it, then. No more neatly folded Jockey® briefs. No more remembering to put the Jet-Dry® in the dishwasher. No more picking through the green beans for the ones that don't have any brown spots.

From now on, I wake up every morning, make an abundance of manly noises in the bathroom, and then strap myself into one of those cool-looking rough-and-tumble cowhide tool belts.

Someone's gonna have to tell me if I've got it on straight, though. That hammer handle seems to be hanging right where it shouldn't be.

HAVE YOU BEEN PICKING BEETS, OR DID YOU JUST COME FROM A GRUBEROVA CONCERT?

Ah, celebrity. Usually it's associated with spotlights, shining performance and glowing reviews. Not all the time, though. We'd probably do well to remember that, way earlier than the time of Dawn (that would be my second-grade girlfriend Dawn Diminski), all the way back to the dawn of time, it's never darker than when the stars come out.

I was reminded of the neurotically unenlightened side of stardom by a recent news report out of Vienna, where Slovak soprano Edita Gruberova celebrated the 45th anniversary of her first stage appearance by performing "La Straniera," a two-act Bellini opera. Just before the show she told an Associated Press reporter that, "If the applause lasts less than 20 minutes, it bothers me."

Well, my God. Who wouldn't be bothered? I insist on an uninterrupted six minutes just for loading the dishwasher. If I were the "queen of coloratura" and my fans weren't willing to lose an epidermal layer or two in recognition of my vocal artistry, I'd be more than just bothered. I probably wouldn't bother at all.

All right. So maybe I wouldn't go that far. OK, OK. The sad truth is, I wouldn't come near to going that far. In fact, my life is so far from going that far that I'd need a passport to even get close.

I'm guessing just about everybody who doesn't routinely get a hand for taking out the garbage or machining a factory part or waiting on a Wendy's® customer who, God help him, should be asking for <u>less</u> Russian dressing, pretty much would agree that 20 minutes of applause is a lot to ask – even if you can hit an E-flat above high C. That probably has to do with the fact that they've been raised to recognize laughable haughtiness, and likely has nothing at all to do with the notion that they're familiar with...

The Parable of the Imperious Tenor

There once was a young man who sang in the shower, just because he was happy and it made him feel good. After several years of steamy practice he became quite good – at singing, that is – and in the warmer months, when the window was open, his neighbors began to recognize his talent.

Among his admirers was a minister who happened to pass by while the young man was laying into "Amazing Grace" (Yes, I see you sniggering), and who immediately signed him up for the church choir. When Christmas arrived and the cathedral rang with the young tenor's heart-stopping "Ave Maria," there wasn't a dry eye in the nave, which triggered an emergency room stampede as parishioners stepped into the sub-zero night and their eyes froze shut.

Soon the young man's reputation spread across the commonwealth and he was asked to sing at the state fair. But something had changed in him. An egotistical veil had descended, darkening his temperament and causing him to think he was superior to everyone else. It was, some said, an unwarranted sense of grandeur... an inferior superiority – perhaps even a posterior superiority, suggestive of equine hindquarters – and his following began to fade.

Then, two days before his scheduled appearance, the young tenor said he wouldn't sing at all unless the audience promised to clap for a full 20 minutes. Choosing preened cows and fattened pigs over a horse's ass, fairgoers by the thousands redeemed their concert tickets for cotton candy and left the singer high and dry. Well, not exactly dry. The rejection drove him to drink, and from that day on he always carried a pint of whiskey in his hip-pocket.

The fallen vocalist managed to piece together a pedestrian career singing on radio ads for a half dozen manufacturers of writing instruments – Parker®, Paper Mate®, BIC® and the like – but the promise of his youth was never realized.

Moral: Get all high and mighty and you'll sing a song of six pens... with a pocketful of rye.

DRESSED FOR EXCESS

Target (department store) apologized for labeling the color of a plus-sized women's dress as "manatee gray" while the same dress in regular sizes was called "dark heather gray." Shoppers slammed the store for what many interpreted as a jab at larger women.

— New York Daily News

"May I help you, madam?"

"Women's Department, please. My friend and I are... 'Helen? Helen! Yoo-hoo! Over here! By the zoology display!' (turning back to the floor assistant)... my friend and I are looking at something stylish for a dinner party later this week."

"Of course. Right this way. Any particular size? I'm guessing petite."

"Why, you rascal, you. 'Helen! (waving now) Here I am, sweetie. We've got a live one!'"

"I'll leave you ladies to your shopping safari. If you have any questions..."

"We'll be fine, thank you. Oh, there is one thing."

"Yes?"

"Will there be bearers to assist with the kill?"

"At your disposal."

"Oh, goody. Did you hear that, Helen?" (who's finally caught up)

"Like a thirty-aught-six in the ladies' room, Roz. Let the hunting begin. Do you see anything in manatee gray?"

"Manatee? (with a twitter). I think you've grossly underestimated the caliber of your shot, Memsahib. Reload, dearie. You're a hippo if I ever saw one."

"Well, aren't you sweet. Are those the African-elephant taupes you're pawing through? Save yourself some time, sister. That beast of a housedress you bought on our last excursion proves your taste is utterly extinct. You ought to be looking at something in a mastodon.

"Ouch. Don't fret, though, Helen dear. That last shot only grazed me. Speaking of grazing, here's a cute little water buffalo brown that looks just right for you."

"See what I mean, Miss Yesterday? Brown is so... Cenozoic. Besides, I've got my crosshairs on that shiny little cerulean number in the rack next to you."

"This one? The whale-blue shift?"

"Goodness, no. What kind of a friend would I be to upset your plans like that? You're going to need that one and the one next to it to cover yourself completely. No. I had something of a lesser cetacean in mind."

"This one? The porpoise-gray? Trust me, Hel. You're going to have to cast a wider net than that. Although they may sell you the entire pod at a discount..."

"Oh, my God, Roz! Have you seen this rhino-gray kimono maxi-dress? It is so you. And I think they'll even let you charge it."

"Touché, bitchkins, but I'm not the embarrassingly horny one here. I saw the moves you put on that barely legal floor-walker – if jiggling blubber counts as movement. Speaking of which... here's a nice little walrus-gray tunic you can sink your tusks into."

"No, that one's definitely for you, sweetie. Nobody's longer in the tooth than you."

"Well, I never!"

"Have been hungrier than you are now?"

"You can read me like a book, Hel."

"More like the Encyclopedia Britannica, buttercup. Shall we see if there's a McDonald's in the food court?"

"Super-size me, sweetheart. Super-size me."

"Like I have any choice..."

HOT LIES, COLD TRUTH

Some people have a nose for the news. Others, it seems, have news for the nose, and into that questionable category recently stumbled the University of Granada. Or was it Grenada? No, it has to be the one in Spain. That tumbledown school on the island Ronnie Reagan picked to showcase America's manhood back in the 1980s barely qualifies as a community college. It may even be a collegial commune. I really don't know.

Where were we, now? Oh, yes. Out of the thermal-imaging labs at the University of Granada comes this warmed-up little morsel: When humans tell a lie, the temperature of their noses goes up. You may think I'm making this up, but I'm not. Here. Put your finger on my nose. I said ON it, wise ass. Don't look at me. It's yours now.

Again. Where were we? Lies. Hot noses. Right. About two sips of coffee worth of interest, you're probably saying, and yesterday I might have agreed. But that was before I saw what I wasn't supposed to see. And, no, I'm not talking about the gardener relieving himself in the rhododendrons.

As it happens, I was at the New York Public Library doing research on attractive women doing research at the New York Public Library, when I quite of a sudden found myself given access to the institution's highly secured Classified Stacks. (My research subjects apparently asked the authorities to detain me long enough to give them a half-hour advantage.) Temporarily imprisoned in an impenetrable room filled with historical arcana that, were it to fall into the wrong hands, might trigger mass public boredom, I decided to while away the time leafing through obscure documentation surreptitiously placed on file by the CIA.

After determining that I was actually looking at a pile of failed recipes from the Culinary Institute of America, I turned my attention to a shelf labeled "NSA–National Security Agency," where I fell privy to the following hand-written logs from an unpublicized experiment performed in 1958. I feel certain that you, the reader, will find them of great interest. And I say that with a very warm nose.

Project Hot Fib

28 May

It begins. Participants – all male – arrive by bus and mule train from across the western region. None of them knows why they're here. Some promised free pizza, but I don't see anything in the budget for that. Most subjects accounted for. No accounting for No. 12, though. How hard could it be to find matching socks?

2 June

Subjects acclimate to specially designed SCUBA masks. Most adapt quickly. No. 12 asks for two – one for each foot. Some have trouble, at first, breathing through their mouths while their noses remain exposed to the water, but come around after demo by Lloyd Bridges, star of "Sea Hunt"

TV show. Actor asks to be informed of go-live date so he can arrange to be on the East Coast.

6 June

Lost four days scrubbing down subjects. (After repeated instructions not to pee in the water, No. 12 relieves himself in tank filled with specially formulated H_2O, chemically altering it. Subjects dyed purple.) Tomorrow = Go Live.

7 June

All subjects successfully outfitted in breathing apparatus and water-proof headphones. Secured at bottom of tank. Test questions begin.

Query 1: "Which one of you rolled up last night's creamed spinach in your napkin?" Subjects look at each other. No acknowledgement from any one participant, but slight temperature variance registered in two-foot radius around No. 12.

Query 2: "Raise your hand if you accurately listed your annual gross income on last year's federal tax form." All lift hands in unison, accompanied by 53-degree rise in overall water temperature. Test engineer expresses some concern about ability of tank to withstand pressure from increase of similar magnitude.

Query 3: "On a manhood scale of 1 to 10, each of you has listed yourself as an 8 or above. Really? All of you?" Every subject nods a furious 'Yes,' but... wait. What's this? Water temperature registering dangerous spike. Approaching boiling point. Oh, my God! Run! Run..!

The log ends abruptly, leaving us without any further hint of the outcome. Did the test subjects survive? And just what was it that caused the experiment to go so catastrophically awry?

Certainly it couldn't have been that last question. I mean, come on. None of us is less than an 8, is he?

Jesus. Is it hot in here, or what?

NO, REALLY. IT WAS JUST A NANO-BIT PART...

IBM said it has made the tiniest stop-motion movie ever – a one-minute video of individual carbon monoxide molecules repeatedly rearranged to show a boy dancing, throwing a ball and bouncing on a trampoline. IBM used a remotely operated two-ton scanning-tunneling microscope at its lab in San Jose, Calif., to make the movie.

— Associated Press

"Orencio!" I shrieked, summoning my man from his usual four-hour espresso break. "Ándelay! I can't find my linens anywhere! Dear lord in heaven... did we leave them in New York?"

"No, *señor*," came the anesthetized reply. "They are here, right before your very outsized and purple-streaked *nariz*."

"Oh, thank God, you worthless excuse for a valet. Ostracism from the human species – perhaps even from Subphylum Vertebrata – was mere seconds away. Why, in this city a man without his whites is nothing but an onlooker – a cultural pariah, unfit for admission to any but the least desirable premieres. I tell you, the mayor of Cannes himself would have escorted me to the airport to ensure my disgraced gluteus maximus was on the next flight out."

"Mayor, *señor*? I think no," his voice dripping with deadly disinterest. "An alderman, perhaps."

"Why, you scoundrel. Fetch me my polka-dot bowtie and Panama hat before I have the hotel management unplug that infernal Wi-Fi you use to maintain constant televised contact with that DeGeneres woman. I'm late for *A Boy and His Atom*."

And with that withering imprecation in my wake, I left, determined to be among the precious few who might lay claim to having a front-row seat at the historic unveiling of International Business Machine's 45-by-25-nanometer entry in the Cannes Film Festival. Certified as the world's smallest stop-motion movie by Guinness World Records, the video reportedly moved individual carbon monoxide molecules into stick-figure positions depicting a boy taking his atomic-scale skateboard out for a spin.

Early reviews of bootlegged copies hailed the 60-second creation for a plot development running the entirety of the human emotional gamut – from antipathy to boredom to head-shaking incredulity at the idea of spending millions of dollars to turn a two-ton scanning-tunneling microscope operating at 450 degrees below zero into a Panaflex®. It was all reportedly there, in 242 frames of cinematic splendor that literally took your breath away – courtesy of dozens of oxygen atoms hijacked to compile an animated figure that could easily disappear down someone's windpipe.

Nestled into my seat at the famed Teatro de Miniscule, I squirmed with anticipation as the house lights dimmed and IBM's tiny hero came to life. Oh, my stars and comets! There he was, his ball-bearing-like physique in nanoscale relief against the nothingness of the quantum vacuum, silver and shining and gliding on molecular dots. Transported by acting that later was variously described as "sublime," "submicroscopic" and "subpoenaed," the enthralled audience stood as one, generating gale-force winds as left hand met right and right hand met left. Some hands left right away, obviously untrained in dealing with the clap.

Unwilling to wait for a determination by the usual panel of judges, the crowd called for an immediate awarding of the prestigious Palme D'Or – scaled, of course, to a size befitting the dimensions of the entry. The prize was graciously accepted by a senior IBM vice president who, intent on protecting the trophy, wrapped it in his handkerchief, but lost it later during a sneezing jag triggered by champagne bubbles.

I was sitting next to him during the outburst, and it may be somewhere in my exquisitely coiffed hair, but I won't know for sure until that damned Orencio finishes examining me with my opera glasses.

IS THAT A YELLOWING... OR A BROWNING?

As is my occasional wont, I was enjoying a civilized breakfast at the local diner, perusing the news in between chews, when my glance landed on a report detailed by Reuters.

An 8-year-old Maryland boy, it seems, had been suspended from elementary school for nibbling his Pop-Tart® into the shape of a gun during snack time. No word on whether it resembled something from the fashionably linear and therefore more easily munched Glock family, or whether it displayed the rather more demanding mandibular artistry required to sculpt, say, a Colt Model 1851 Navy.

Confronted with the wussy truth that I had never handled either one, and in fact was much more adept at juggling a fork, my attention returned to my eggs and the smiling waitress who had materialized next to me, coffee pot in hand.

"Got everything you need, hon'?" she inquired.

"*Oui, mon cheri,*" I replied, raising a napkin to make my lips more kissable. "These fried beauties were over easier than my first love affair. Frieda was her name, as I recall, and..."

"Wait a minute," she interrupted, pointing to my plate, "What's that?"

"What's what?"

"That yellow thing."

Puzzled for a picosecond, I quickly surmised that her attention was riveted on the fanciful puddle left by what remained of my broken fast. "Why, it's a yolk stain, my dear. Surely you're familiar with..."

"It's a gun," she said, stepping back, her voice drained of the sunshine that had earlier suffused it.

"I beg your pardon?"

"It's a gun," she repeated, louder now, eyes darting left and right, as if in search of reinforcements.

"Well," I granted on second look, "I suppose if you turn it this way, it does sort of resemble..."

"Oh, my God. He's pointing it at me. He's pointing it at me! Manny!!"

And before I could dab my toast in the damning evidence, Manny was upon us. "Are you all right, Carly? What's going on here?" he demanded.

"My good man, er... Manny," I stuttered, "there is absolutely nothing going on here. This woman nonsensically accuses me of..."

"Jesus! Is that a gun?"

Sensing an unfavorable momentum, I paused, took a deep breath and calmly reached for my plate. "As you can plainly see," I admonished in my most teacherly tone, "this is a yolk stain..."

"Sir," Manny instructed, "I'm going to have to ask you to keep your hands away from the dishware. T-h-a-t's right. T-h-a-t's right," he instructed. "Put your hands on your seat and sit on them.

If you know what's good for you, you won't make any sudden moves. Chuck!" he shouted. "Chuck! Dial 911."

———————

After 20 minutes of questioning and a table-top demonstration of fluid dynamics conducted by the short-order cook, the police began to soften, and I'm fairly certain I would have escaped if I hadn't accidentally up-ended the catsup bottle on my way out.

Damned if that spill didn't look exactly like a Howitzer.

CALL ME LIPSCHUTZ

Given the sensitivity of the topic, I wasn't going to say anything about that story out of New Zealand. You know – the one in the *Otago Daily Times* about the lady who mistook super glue for lip balm and sealed her lips shut.

Damn good rag, the *Times*. That Sunday section on awkward moments with kiwis deserves some serious Pulitzer attention. I mean, who would guess they'd even fit in some of those places.

Anyway, if nothing else, silence probably would have been the poetically appropriate response to the glue story, but you know how things go. The wheels start spinning, the scenes start weaving themselves together and suddenly it's too late. Which is why you now find yourself subjected to this delicate little gem, manifested as I envisioned the kind of conversation that might occur as a woman who had just super-glued her lips together tried to get the attention of her husband, whose head is buried in the morning newspaper.

It started out as dialogue, but the way it developed, it probably would be more accurately classified as soliloquy. Shall we listen in? Do we have a choice? Not if you expect to get through the day without discovering a kiwi where it shouldn't be.

Mmmphh!

"G'morning."

Nnnh, nnnh. Mmmphh!

"Nah... not today. Stomach's a little on edge. I think I'll have oatmeal. Raisins would be good."

Kkupf! (snort) Kkupf!

"If you're pouring yourself some, sure."

Unh unh! Unh... unh!

"Slept pretty good, I guess. Had to get up once."

Luh aaa mmuh, ooo oreh aaphh! Ay kknt taw!

"Oh, yeah. Sorry. Must have been the sauerkraut."

(a muffled whimper)

(looks up briefly) "Geez... I said I was sorry! We were out of Tums.® (returns to the sports page) Low on paper towels, too. You going to the A&P today?"

(resigned sobbing)

"Yeah. We could use some of those, too, I guess."

Heph eee, eez!

"You don't say."

(slaps forehead)

"He had it coming, I guess. (turning to the business section) Listen. I got your mother that jumbo roll of electrician's tape she asked for, but I want it to be a surprise for her birthday, so don't say anything."

Huh? Eee nnt ahk or ape...

"Sure she did. Remember when she complained it would be a shock to her system if I ever got her anything useful? (glances up) Well, I love your mom and wouldn't want anything to happen to her, so I bought her some tape. (folds the paper and gets up to leave) Guess I better hit the road. Big meeting today. (gives her a good-bye kiss followed by an odd look). Damn, Doris. Your breath could take out the Fifth Regiment. Better pick up some mouthwash, too."

Oooate!

(phone rings just as he opens the front door) "Speak of the devil. Bet that's your mom now. Remember. It's a birthday gift, so don't say anything."

———————————

She didn't.

JUST SWIMMINGLY, THANK YOU

A large group of exhibitionists went for a swimsuit-free dip in the Mediterranean Sea in a bid to break the skinny-dipping world record. The 729 nude swimmers were apparently successful, surpassing the previous record. According to the Europa Press, Vera (Spain) Mayor José Carmelo Jorge was pleased with the turnout, calling the mass nude swim a tremendous success.

— Huffington Post

One moment, if you would. I'm in the midst of a very important phone call and shan't be able to take your questions. I've just rung up the mayor of Vera, Spain, you see, and I...

"Yes, hello? May I speak with the mayor, please? Oh, I see. It <u>is</u> you, then. Well, a very good afternoon to you, Mr. Mayor. I'm calling all the way from New York and... Why, yes. I'm afraid it is unpleasantly warm. Dirty little trick, this climate change phenomenon, don't you think? Costing my wife hundreds in dress shields. Oh, my. Well, that would be quite generous of you, really, but I think she'll get on nicely with her own supply.

"The reason for my call is that there appears to have been committed a social faux pas of considerable proportions. Yes, of course. I'd be glad to. It seems that a record-setting nude swim party was hosted in your fine city recently, and Mildred and I never received an invitation. Oversight? Well, I would say it was enormously more than that, Mr. Jorge. By the way, that is your last name, am I correct? Good. It is a touch confusing, after all. One usually presumes Jorge to be a first name. Odd sort of ancestral line, don't you think? Half expecting your first name to be Menendez. Hah, hah! Bit of ribbing there, old man.

"Now, as I was saying, I would think it was a tad more than simple oversight, Jorge. Sorry. Mister Jorge. Damn awkward bit of nonsense, that naming policy. What _is_ your first name, if I may ask? José? I see. Would you be terribly offended if I used that, then? Wonderfully decent of you.

"Now, where were we? Yes, well I'm afraid oversight simply won't do, my good man. Mildred and I are privileged to be on some of the most elite invitation lists in the world, and to find ourselves excluded from an event of such obvious social consequence, well... it's just not done, Jorge. Mister Jorge. All right then, José.

"Yes, I am completely aware. More than 700 participants... yes, I know. But that's just my point, don't you see? Mildred and I are among 'the four hundred,' my dear chap, which makes a formal invitation de rigueur, wouldn't you think?

"No recognizable figures of high standing? Well, I would beg to differ, my good Mister José. Look here. All we need do is examine the wire photo accompanying the news article. Do you have yours? Oh. Right. Framed already, is it? Well, then... you'll have no difficulty following me up to the extreme left... three rows back. Yes, I believe you've got it. Those are without a doubt the withered bosoms of Mrs. Phillip Winthrop Cavendish III. I would know them anywhere. And there, in front, between the inner tube and that

gaily colored orb. Yes, well, I suppose they do call them beach balls. Right there in the middle. That stunning appendage most assuredly belongs to Cecil Kensington, owner of the world-famous Kensington Miming Dimes. I beg your pardon? Oh, did I? Well, I meant Diamond Mines, of course. It must be that peculiar pose he's struck. Looks like he's stuck in a box, doesn't it?

"Yes, well... I know it's too late to make amends for this particular event, but I've cobbled together an absolutely over-the-top idea to set things straight. Brilliant, really. Virtually guaranteed to garner front-page coverage. All it requires is a helpful telephone call from you to your counterpart in Pamplona. A sort of professional favor, if you will. Right. Well, you've guessed it exactly, now, haven't you?

"A fashionably nude Running of the Bulls. You have our address."

Birthday Suit

The nicest gift, of course, would have been if the damned *Louisville Courier-Journal* hadn't published the story in the first place. But there it was, available for anyone with two dollars in his pocket. **Lawsuit: Who Wrote 'Happy Birthday'?** the front-page banner read. No indication, of course, about the subsequent homicide-induced headlines that snappy little teaser was bound to generate.

To be fastidiously fair, though, I suppose the ensuing mayhem could be traced all the way back to those degenerate siblings Mildred and Patty, of the venerable Louisville Hill family, to whom the song has been attributed all these years, and to whose designated assignees nearly $2 million per annum in licensing payments has been flowing like a catchy tune. Apparently, the idea that party-goers should be hit with royalty fees every time they warble what is arguably the most frequently sung song in the English language is offensive to some, to the extent that a federal lawsuit has been filed calling for its relegation to the no-cost public domain.

Well, if it please the court, a few pennies stipend would have been a singularly small price to pay to side-step what in local folklore has quickly come to be known as Marge Bargewaller's Unhappy Birthday— a.k.a. The Spatula Incident. It is only with great trepidation and a fear of unspeakable reprisals that I relate to you the following *chronologie somber*.

The Bargewallers, it seems, are the sworn enemies of the Hills. Been that way for years, I'm told. Something to do with a pair of borrowed pruning shears never properly returned and, what was it? Oh, yes... a borrowed fiancée, also never properly returned. They are Louisville's version of the Hatfields and McCoys, with the minor difference that their weapons of choice are the weekly social columns and snide comments overheard each Sunday in the echoing sacristy of the Church of the Occasional Resurrection – the preferred house of worship for local bankers, furriers and contract bridge champions.

It would have been nice if someone had said something. As it was, I showed up at Marge's 63rd birthday attired in blissful ignorance and a matching bowtie, urged by my butcher to make an appearance on his behalf as I passed the Bargewaller mansion on my way to a South American archeological dig. What can I say. The man's pinwheel flank steaks are works of art.

After the requisite exchange of pleasantries – "Well, I can't believe it. For a family with old money, yours doesn't look a day over 30. Are those real diamonds in the champagne flutes?" – a crowd gathered for the unveiling of the cake, which, as we all know, is the universal signal to break out in song. So I did.

"Happy birthday to..." Mine being the only voice in evidence, I stopped short. "Sorry," I said, aware suddenly that every iris in the room had narrowed in my direction. "Wrong key? Let's try something lower then, say... in F." And I started up again, lifting my hands, maestro-like, to encourage participation. "Happy birthday to you..."

My musical tribute was interrupted once again, this time by a man later identified as the Bargewaller's accountant. "I say, old man. Do shut up, will you? You'll cost the family a small fortune."

"I beg your pardon?"

"The residuals, man. Royalties. Damned if we'll turn one more penny over to those blood-sucking Hills." There was a moment of pensive silence, and then the soft background sobbing of the birthday girl gave way to gang indignity.

"Wait a minute," someone inquired. "Who is this guy?"

"Yeah, who is he, anyway?"

"Never seen him before."

"Oh, my God. He's a Hill! He's a Hill!"

Sensing that the Hills were something I should immediately take to, I made for the front door. Burdened by the weight of burning candles and frosting rosettes, I was unable to move quickly enough, however, to avoid being slapped on the cheek with the silver spatula Marge had been using to deftly dismember her five-layered masterpiece.

The redness had nearly faded when, two weeks later, I managed to unearth a heretofore undiscovered line of Incan script at the base of a temple in the lost city of Macchu Picchu. It took another fortnight to have it translated.

"Happy birthday to you," it read. "Happy birthday to you."

IN PARENTIS LOCO

No matter how hard they try to assert their independence, most people are destined to "turn into" their parents. Polling by Netmums, the parenting website, identified the age of 32 as the point at which people are most likely to have crossed the line from rebellious youth to being a younger copy of their own mother or father.

— The Telegraph

It was on the uptown bus, somewhere between Macy's and 42nd Street, when I turned into my father. I know this because I took my seat dressed in jeans and a stylish Armani t-shirt, and when I got off I was wearing seersucker pants and a bowtie.

The experience probably would have thrown most people for a psychodynamic loop, but I had just come from a marathon showing of *The Matrix* trilogy at the Palace and presumed several synapses on the left side of my brain hadn't sufficiently reset. Ironically, it all became clear when, stepping off the curb at Vanderbilt Avenue, I suddenly developed presbyopia and was forced to stop at Duane-Reade pharmacy for reading glasses.

There was no denying it. I was undergoing parental transmogrification.

Fighting an urge to light up a Camel®, I took a right onto Third Avenue and walked south in the direction of Locks & Lox, a barber shop and smoked fish emporium founded by my family back in the '50s. All well and good, of course, unless you take into consideration that I'm a phlebotomist – a bloody good one, at that – and work at a walk-in clinic across from the United Nations. I turned on a heel (he was making fun of an elderly woman whose stockings had fallen around her ankles) and headed north, pondering the gravity of my circumstance.

"How had this happened?" I wondered, raising my hand to scratch my head, only to be thwarted by the presence of a brown fedora that, from the standpoint of fashionability, didn't go with anything I was wearing.

An adenoidal "Oy vey!" floated from my throat before I could do anything about it, and the waistband of my pants mysteriously levitated to a spot just beneath my pectorals. Luckily, my argyle socks remained in place, secured by an attractive pair of red garters.

It was only at a newsstand near Ralph Bunche Park that I was struck by the cosmic seriousness of my predicament, shaken from my stupor by a frightening impulse to ignore *Playboy* in favor of a Brookings Institution report titled *Central Banks in the New World of Unconventional Monetary Policy*.

"Are you meshuggina?" I asked myself. A reply was out of the question, of course, since I had no idea what the word meant. What I did know was that my very soul was at stake, and if I wanted to remain the man I was – despite his inability to process milk products – I had to fight back. From that point on I resisted every inducement to become my father. Wait! Was that the smell of beef brisket emanating from Leftwich's Deli? "No!" I silently screamed. "Run, you fool. Run!"

Covering my nose and mouth with the ridiculous headwear that had materialized on my now balding pate, I sprinted past every sound, every smell, every human interaction that might incent me to react in the manner of the man who had brought me into this world 32 years ago. Miraculously fending off the urge to shout "son of a bitches," I rounded the corner at East 44th and First and staggered into the walk-in clinic, where, after several cups of coffee made from organically grown beans, I slowly began to recover.

This was my world, and with each successive patient I regained more of the man I knew I was. By the end of the day I had completely returned, reconstituted down to my jeans and my Armani shirt. There were moments, of course, when the threat of relapse arose, not the least of which occurred when the office radio was accidentally tuned to a station playing the Ray Conniff Singers. With quick thinking, I managed to survive. The fire alarm can be replaced, after all. I cannot.

Fully regenerated, at day's end I bid my coworkers a fond good evening and caught the downtown bus for home. I was back.

It was somewhere between 32nd Street and Gramercy Park, I believe – shortly after I found myself reaching under my collar to adjust a phantom bra strap – that I turned into my mother.

SOCK IT TO ME

I collapsed in a weeping heap, dabbing joyful tears with the ragged boxer shorts that had saved me. I was still in the game. Still in the game...

(22 minutes earlier)

The words sprang from the page like miniature pogo sticks, ricocheting off my retinas and lodging in a small cranial compartment labeled Stinging Disbelief. "No," I whimpered. "It cannot be!"

Struggling to free my considerable hindquarters from the exercise-free comfort of a club chair, I rose to the call of incredulity, scattering newsprint to the four winds of my study... and simultaneously vowing to have someone attend to the weather stripping around the window.

In my barely perceptible wake (curse those considerable hindquarters), page four of *The Telegraph* fluttered to the floor, its heart-stopping headline landing faceup. **Man Claims to Own Oldest Socks in Britain**, it declared, offering as indisputable evidence the following script:

Frank Tunbridge of Podsmead, Gloucester, claimed his socks are the oldest in regular use in Britain because he has been wearing them every weekend for the last 25 years. He said he has walked hundreds of miles in them, and only recently has the first hole appeared. "The funny thing is that I bought another pair of the same socks at the time and they didn't last anywhere near as long as this pair."

There was nothing funny about it. Nothing in the least. For I, I was the true and bona fide owner of the oldest stockings in Britain, and sometime subsequent to the 21 minutes it would take for me to ascend the staircase to my second-floor armoire, I would produce them for the clamoring press.

"Why, the very idea..," I muttered, growing more indignant with each minute-and-a-half step. Members of the peerage from Exmouth to Northumberland – all intimately familiar with the 800-year bloodline of my Clan Douglas argyles – would surely step forward to testify on their behalf. From Hastings to the plains of Boulogne, they had graced the ankles of kings and queens alike (there remains some conjecture about whether Elizabeth I was a man or a woman), establishing them as the uncontested socks of the realm. "Twenty-five years, indeed!" I ranted.

Breathless with contempt, I paused at the top of the stairs to regain my bearings and proceeded to the dressing room, determined to set the record straight with one swift pull of the sock drawer. "Here!" I shouted triumphantly, separating the whites from the darks in wild anticipation of righting an abominable wrong. "Walk a mile in these, you miserable..." With a piercing gasp, I inhaled what remained of my imprecation. They weren't there. England's oldest socks weren't there!

Panicked, I sought spousal assistance. "Hilde!" I bellowed. "Hilde!"

"What is it, Reginald? Can't you see I'm on a roll with *Wheel of Fortune*?"

"My blue argyles. I can't find my blue argyles!"

"Oh, those ratty old things. You asked me to darn them, but I damned them instead. Dropped them in a Salvation Army clothes box and picked you up some spiffy new over-the-calves at Harrods."

My chin dropped to the sweater level, two drawers down, as I pondered the chilling historical ramifications of my wife's folly. "They're... they're gone," I sobbed. "Britain's oldest socks... gone."

My reputation now as unraveled as my precious stockings, I contemplated self-imposed banishment to the American Midwest. I had Cunard Lines on the phone, in fact, sympathizing with my descent from peerage to steerage, when it struck me with the force of one of those tools I've never had to use – a slammer, or hammer, or something like that.

England's oldest underlinens! Snatched from a Norman clothesline in 1267 and passed down from generation to generation! Could they still be in my underwear drawer? Crazed with hope, I yanked the wooden trough from its moorings, emptied its contents into a pile on the bed and rummaged through them like a madman.

Fruit of the Loom? No! *Jockey?* Never! *Walmart?* Oh, dear God, man. What were you thinking? And then suddenly – miraculously – my hands closed around them, lustrous and pink and frail with age.

"Yes!" I cried. "Yes! Yes, oh yes!"

The oldest underpants in Britain.

THE (SUSPICIOUS) THING WITH FEATHERS

An Egyptian man performed a citizen's arrest on a swan, taking it to police on suspicion of being a spy. The man suspected the bird was an undercover agent because it carried an electronic device. (Officials) thought it likely to be a wildlife tracker. Earlier this year, a security guard filed a police report after capturing a pigeon he said carried microfilm reels... and in July a kestrel was detained in Turkey on suspicion of being an Israeli spy.

– The Telegraph

"Name?"

"El Pato Donald. Some call me Donald Le Canard. To others, I am Дональд дак."

"So. You wish to play games. Tell me this, my half-naked friend: If Walt Disney walked into this interrogation room right now, what might he call you?"

"Waaak! (laughingly) I see you have done your homework, *mon inspecteur*."

"It is true, then. You are the notorious Donald Duck. A little far from home, aren't you?"

"Depends. Hollywood can be a bit, shall we say... unexciting nowadays. Pants and shoes everywhere, I'm afraid. So trite. So... conformist. Besides, I have business here in Cairo."

"Yes, I imagine you do. And may I ask what that might be?"

"My, my. Full of interrogatories, aren't we?"

"I question that."

"Hmm. Well, my dear inspector, without revealing too much about what are, in fact, my private affairs, let us say that I remain in the ... heh, heh... film business."

"Of course, Mr. Duck, of course. And given the incredibly small size of the reels we confiscated from your nephews, would it be fair to conclude that your career has taken a precipitous turn for the worse and you are now accepting... how to put this delicately... microscopically small parts?"

"Waaak! My nephews? What have you done with them, you scoundrel!"

"Let's just say that Huey and Dewey won't be in attendance during the next 20 years' worth of Junior Woodchuck meetings."

"And Louie?"

"I'm sorry, El Pato, but it is indeed a dangerous pond in which you paddle. Your nephew Louie, I'm afraid, made what proved to be fatal contact with... *sauce à l'orange*."

(After several seconds of silence) "I see. (Several more seconds of silence) Do you think, *mon inspecteur*, that I might have a cigarette?"

"But of course (extending a pack), although our brands are mostly American now."

"You are aware, then, that I favor Turkish tobacco?"

"All too well, Mr. Duck. It was, in fact, your recent activity in Turkey that put us on your trail."

"Well, then. It would appear that the game (laughing at his own ironic reference to hunted animals)... is up!"

"Quite."

"And what is to become of me now, my dear inspector?"

(Standing and making ready to leave) "You will be deported to your place of residence in America."

"Hollywood?"

"North Hollywood, I believe."

"But... but that's no place for an international star. That's where they make those god-awful porn flicks!"

"A fitting venue, I'm sure (turning as he exits)... for one so adamantly without pants."

GODDAMN THE GROCER MAN

Oreos are as addictive as cocaine, at least for lab rats, and just like us, they like the creamy center best. Eating the sugary treats activates more neurons in the brain's 'pleasure center' than drugs such as cocaine, a team at Connecticut College found.

— NBC News

My name is Delbert Sweetman, and I'm an Oreo-aholic. I've been Oreo-free for three hours, 22 minutes and 14 seconds—15 now— and I may relapse if the woman next to me wearing the black-and-white horizontal striped sweater doesn't leave the room.

Thank you, ma'am. I'd also appreciate it if the rest of you would discontinue munching on packaged foods during my confession. The sound of crinkling plastic has been known to weaken my resolve. I'm sorry, what? No one here is snacking? Then I can only conclude that someone in the group needs a desperate change of underwear. No, no... not now, sir! Please. Retake your seat.

Mine is a story that, I'm sure, will be familiar to everyone here. Except maybe for the part about the turkey baster. I'm told that's a fairly unique practice. Those who are curious can visit my website at www. wow_that's_cold, where I've posted several jpegs.

The real trouble began in 1981, when as a mere kindergartener I was introduced to the diabolical delights of Oreo chocolate sandwich cookies by Lester Storrbawt, whose mother apparently hadn't the necessary family recipes to produce her own baked goods. Oh, she tried, God love her, but when your orange-cranberry loaves ultimately find utility as foundation blocks, well... there isn't much impetus to please, is there? From that point on, Lester became my pusher, slowly ushering my descent into Nabisco hell.

At first I was able to control my desire for the crème-filled biscuits, deferring consumption under pretense of the unavailability of the proper accompanying libation. "Cookie?" Lester the Snake would ask, innocently reaching into his lunch bag. "No," I would reply with a wan smile. "There's no milk to go with it." But you don't get to be a cookie pusher without possessing the street-smarts to recognize world-class junkie potential like me, and Lester, well... Lester knew just how to flick my switch. First it was Oreos with Coke®. Then Oreos with water. Before I knew it, I was mainlining the chocolate tabs, snarfing them down on spit alone, one after the debilitating other.

I was hooked.

My friends? Oh, they kept trying to tell me, of course. But as it is with every cookie addict, I was in denial. "The creamy center holds no special attraction for me," I protested. "Look. I can eat it whole!" But I couldn't. So crazed was I that, every night for hours, I would practice unscrewing the cookie with my tongue and licking the frosting clean, all under cover of a closed mouth. Needless to say, my coursework suffered – especially Public Speaking.

The low point came in July, when, in my madness, I stole a double-stuffed from a toddler and tried to snort it whole. Badly misjudging the malleability of my left nostril, I dropped the biscuit, leaving behind trace samples of DNA that ultimately put the police on my trail. I was arrested and prosecuted, and following a guilty plea was sentenced to an extended period of rehabilitation, which includes regular attendance here at Oreo-aholics Anonymous.

As you can imagine, I have been shunned by friends and family—the toddler in question was my nephew Ridley—and my progress has been painfully slow. As of late, however, I have begun to sense a slight lifting of the darkness and... Oh, my God. I've just peeled off another cookie top, haven't I?

Well, then. It would seem the road to rehabilitation is never-ending. Perhaps, for the sake of all of us, it would be best if I were escorted back to my room. Would someone be so kind as to notify our hostess?

Wait. Did I say... Hostess®?

FOLLICLE SUB NOSA

Full disclosure: This year, I'm not in the running.

Fuller disclosure: I've never been in the running.

I'm talking, of course, about the annual contest for the Robert Goulet Memorial Mustached American of the Year Award, a tonsorially elite face-off sponsored by a wry but very real organization called the American Mustache Institute.

If you're more familiar with living Lady Gagas than you are with dead Goulets, Bob (Yes, we were on a first-name basis; if somebody as famous as him had actually known mine, it would have been a first.) was a barrel-throated singer and actor whose voice, trademark mustache, sense of humor and black leather jackets represented what the institute calls "a quadruple threat of talent." He also represented Canada, the official land of his birth, which sort of leaves you scratching your head about why he was selected to epitomize the very best of mustachioed Americans. Unless they mean North Americans.

I mean, come on. For a truly iconic U.S. mustache, how can you beat the homeland beauty sported by Groucho Marx? It was thick and full and lustrously black... and 100 percent fake. Here in America, we don't want our mustaches dripping with testosterone. We want them dripping with paint.

But, once again, I'm not in the running. And it's not for want of a brush and a bucket of Benjamin Moore. It's because the married woman I'm seeing – OK, so maybe she's my wife – says a mustache makes me look older... and I suppose by association, less attractive. I'm not so sure she's thought that position completely through, though, since no matter how it makes me look, there's the off chance that it makes <u>her</u> look a tad ageist. Either that or she's afraid if I look too old, people won't think she's sexy enough to attract younger men.

However, truth in advertising – along with a second off chance that photons from this little composition might actually collide with my wife's lovely eye bulbs – compels me to announce that neither of those propositions is the least bit accurate. My better half is notably open-minded and, to my reasonably open mind, still quite beautiful. Which leads me to guess the real reason she's not too hot on the idea of me growing a 'stache' is that she doesn't like Cheerios all that much, and suspects that somewhere in the rambling thicket beneath my nostrils she'd run into the remnants of one or two when she's kissing me.

And she's probably right. Whether it's minestrone or a relationship, lip hair has the capability of straining just about anything.

All of which leads me to this final and fullest of disclosures: Even if I decided that an extended period of kissless-ness was a realistic option, I still wouldn't be in the running for Mustached American of the Year, simply as a matter of spelling preference.

I mean, really. How can refinement of any measure be assigned to an organization that would deliberately trim the 'o' out of moustache? It makes me want to cry.

And when I cry my nose runs.

Luckily for my wife, I don't have a mustache.

Neither rain nor snow nor undertow…

The world's oldest message in a bottle may have been found in Canada, discovered by a man as he explored a beach on Vancouver Island. (He) said he was able to discern cursive lettering without opening the bottle, even identifying an apparent signature dated Sept. 29, 1906. The envelope noted the bottle was thrown overboard 76 hours into an ocean trip from San Francisco to Bellingham, Wash. (The man who found it) maintains he won't be opening it any time soon.

– Huffington Post

Boy, a Martini would hit the spot right about now. Let's see. Where's that new liter of gin? Oh, yeah. Right here next to the... Jesus! (crash) Oh, my stars and little comets! My message in a bottle! Damn these big hands. I don't care if they do telegraph a disproportionately prodigious manhood.

Now what? People have been pestering me for years about what was inside, and I just gave them that ridiculously inscrutable smile—like somehow I already knew the wondrous secrets sealed in the bottle and didn't need to crack it open. Man, I can't tell you how many dates that little come-on has gotten me.

Oh, well. Kinda sad, really (sigh)... but I suppose every bottle needs to break. Although that doesn't mean Mona's off the hook for dropping the Beefeater's® last week. I told her there'd be trouble if she took it in the shower with her.

Might as well see what the note says. Where the hell are the olives, anyway?

*   *   *

Sept. 29, 1906

Whoever finds this, I'd appreciate it if you could call Dr. Gutzman and let him know I won't be able to make my appointment next Tuesday. He'll bill me anyway, the schmuck, but given my current circumstance he'll have a heck of a time trying to collect.

You'll excuse me if by the tenor of my last words I seem to suggest that my fiancée, Juanita Rosenblatz of the Ghirardelli chocolate Rosenblatzes (Don't ask; it's obvious there was some seriously disturbing cross-pollination going on there), is in any way responsible for our predicament. Let me be clear. She absolutely is.

"Bellingham, Washington?" I said. "What's there for us besides damp underwear and nasal congestion? Let's stay here in San Francisco," I said. "It's a statistical impossibility we'll be hit by two earthquakes in the same year." Besides, I reminded her, they're finally getting around to having a fire sale at Gump's. But no. Apparently one disaster wasn't enough. Before I knew it we were occupying a stateroom on the Canine Pile, a steamer, leaving 'Frisco in our wake.

Three days out, the Pile came to a shuddering halt. There was a terrible groaning sound, which turned out to be the couple in the cabin next door, either enjoying connubial bliss or paying the price for a bad batch of clams. Seconds later a ship-shaking explosion tore a hole in the aft section, just below the waterline. (I mean, come on. Who locates a septic collection tank right over the boiler?)

We're listing precipitously to the right, but it really doesn't matter. I doubt we'll ever see another voting booth. In 20 minutes I'll be bobbing out there with the trunks and the sex toys. Wow. Look at 'em all. Guess it wasn't the clams.

To the untrained eye it probably will seem like I'm fluttering my legs in a desperate attempt to stay afloat, but actually I'll be kicking myself for taking a pass on those swimming lessons at the local 'Y.' Hey. Eight bucks seemed like a lot at the time, you know?

Anyway, before I go I want to share a vision I've just had. It looks like an apple with a bite taken out of it, and I don't know why, but I think it has something to do with a market. Not the kind you find at Fisherman's Wharf, though. A new kind, where you don't eat or wear the stuff you buy.

I know it sounds strange, but whatever the hell these things are, I'd buy a lot of 'em if I were you.

LET'S SEE THOSE PEARLY WHITES... OR ELSE

A study in Personality and Social Psychology Bulletin *found that high-powered people smiled (only) when they felt happy. The findings suggest that powerful people have the privilege of smiling when they please, whereas those with less power are obligated to smile in order to ingratiate themselves.*

Fighting is about dominance, and smiles may inadvertently signal that a person is less dominant, hostile or aggressive, researchers reported in the journal Emotion.

– NBC Today show

(from an imagined Broadway musical adaptation of Donald Trump's TV show *The Apprentice*)

(Sung to the tune of "Smile," by Charlie Chaplin)

Smile while I keep you waiting,
As you're ingratiating,
While you perform
For the suits... lick my boots.

If you smile even though you hate to,
Smile while I dominate you,
I may just keep you on my staff...
For laughs.

Smile just to keep me sated.
I don't feel obligated.
Why should I try when it's plain
I can buy...

One and then... keep your pay from clearing.
Smile. Yours keeps disappearing.
Don't make me call the payroll guys.
Get wise.

You, who have lousy credit,
Smile, just because I said it.
Don't even think
About frowning, you dink.

If you smile I may not demote you.
Smile... and I may promote you.
Give me a nice shit-eating grin
And you may win.

SHARK BIT

This will be news to nobody: These days, you can find anything you want on the Web. Romance, lab rats, nose rings, raunch, righteousness and recipes for both dinner and disaster. It's all there. You can even find the National Security Agency finding you finding anything you want. Disturbing, yes, but not altogether unexpected.

What used to be *extraordinaire* is now *phénomène normal*, and it's precisely that reformulation of what's "usual" that set my cultural antennae buzzing recently when an accidental mistyping of a particularly onerous URL misdirected me into the dark recesses of prime-time television programming. When you think you've seen it all and then stumble over an item of such surpassing excess that the phrase "you ain't seen nuthin' yet" actually underperforms, you know you're on to something big.

In this case, big translates into little-known on a massive scale. Its hugeness derives from a Herculean effort to make it small, in such a way that tiny becomes enormous. In other words, you know it's big when it's this little. All right, somebody stop me. There's a vial of white pills in the top drawer. Yes, right there... next to the beef jerky and the nylon stockings. Thank you.

Now then, where were we? Oh, yeah. Suppressed television programming. By pure digital happenstance (OK, so maybe a sizeable aperitif was involved) I uncovered part of a long-lost script for a TV pilot that was obviously destined to become ABC's hit show *Shark Tank* – you know... where a bunch of nobodies pitch their get-rich-quick schemes to millionaire tycoons, hoping to pry loose some start-up capital. Now that I think about it, it wasn't so much a pilot as a ground service mechanic, and I base that on content that, as you are about to see, never really gets airborne.

*   *   *

Scene 1: A clearly dazzled man wearing a sock hat, Bermuda shorts and combat boots is ushered into a plush 35th-floor business suite, where he is introduced to four well-dressed executives sitting in posh, umbrian leather chairs: a deceased but easily recognizable fried-chicken magnate; the CEO of a nationwide chain of falafel stands; the owner of a company that manufactures coal-fired space shuttles, and a U.S. senator who, through creative legislative amendments, has managed to steer $6 billion in farm subsidies to an asparagus plant in his backyard.

Falafel CEO: Welcome. Why are you here today?

Contestant: Well, I had this idea, see, for a franchise called Half Ass. It combines gyms where you get weight training with low-fat food regimens. You know... join for a monthly fee, and when you leave you have half the ass you had when you signed up.

Falafel CEO: Brilliant! We'll locate them in every major city, right next to stores specializing in organic produce. Whole Foods and Half Ass. I love it!

Rocket Tycoon: Hey, wait a minute. I want a piece of this, too. I'll give you three-quarters of a million for one-third ownership in Half Ass.

Senator: I'm thinking healthcare funding here...

Chicken Magnate: (utter silence)

Scene 2: A well-coiffed woman wearing an expensive pantsuit and carrying a brushed aluminum briefcase enters an ultra-modern board room, at the center of which is a priceless redwood conference table. Around it are positioned four people: a software billionaire whose claim to fame is a smartphone app that purports to disable every other smartphone app if you don't buy it; a Wall Street mogul who made his fortune shorting elevator shoes; a Big Pharma tycoon whose company markets tap water as an odorless pheromone guaranteed to attract the opposite sex; and a janitor who wasn't able finish his chores before the meeting began. The woman puts her briefcase on the table, opens it with a dramatic flourish and pulls out a small piece of injection-molded plastic.

Contestant: Gentlemen, I give you the Holy Grail of children's toys. I can make 'em for a nickel and sell 'em for $1.79.

Wall Street Guy: Hold on a second. Lemme see that. I think I had one of those when I was a kid.

Drug Big Wig: Yeah. Me, too. Come on, lady. It's a stinkin' nose flute!

Contestant: True, but this one is tuned to F-sharp...

Software Magnate: All right. So maybe you've got our attention now.

Contestant: ... and during the manufacturing process (pauses for effect) it's impregnated with antibiotics.

Drug Big Wig: Whoa! You mean you can play this thing all day and never catch a cold?

Janitor: I'm in.

        *   *   *

Actually, he wasn't. Notes scribbled in the margins make it clear that he was escorted in just the opposite direction – out.

Two days later, pondering the fleeting nature of fame, he found the script in a pile of papers waiting to be recycled and quickly scheduled a visit to a competing network.

Either You're Aphorism or You're Not

I was standing in the shower the other day when it struck me. Well, actually two things struck me. The first was a freshly opened bar of soap left precariously balanced on a bottle of shampoo by the squeaky clean house goddess who had preceded me. (Hey. If the choice is being bonked with a bar of Lifebuoy or being laved alone, I'll take the bonking.) The second thing that struck me was this pithy notion: In the accelerated throes of the 21st-century, quick decisions are an ironic impossibility. There's just too damn much information out there to evaluate.

Consider, for example, what used to be a fairly straightforward purchase. Buying jeans? Excellent! Just answer a few questions if you don't mind. Stone-washed or natural? Button fly or zipper? Easy-fit, regular, slim or emaciated? Whole, unblemished fabric or fashionably distressed? Precisely how much kneecap would you like exposed?

And look at how we've managed to complicate interpersonal relations. Boss giving you a hard time? Nowadays a reasonable employee doesn't just quit. No, he assesses all the possible extenuating circumstances. Does this particular executive, for example, suffer from some variant of gastro-esophageal reflux disease? Is her husband cheating on her? Did the folks at Bloomingdale's complicate things a little by announcing (in only the most sensitive way) that she'd graduated to a size 16? Is her Prozac bumping up against her Abilify? So much—so very much— to process and evaluate before filing charges.

I blame the Internet, of course—a place where you can get electron-fast access to a galaxy of irrelevant data punched out by personality-disordered schmucks who want desperately to influence somebody—anybody—into spending a few picoseconds with them. Everybody is an expert... and so, of course, nobody is an expert.

What we need to counteract all this complexity, I think, is a return to epigrams—short, sage sayings recognized as much for their guiding light and common sense as their wit. You know. Stuff like Ben Franklin used to scribble in *Poor Richard's Almanack.* "After three days men grow weary of a wench, a guest and weather rainy." "A light purse is a heavy curse." "As pride increases, fortune declines." And of course the indefatigable "Early to bed and early to rise, makes a man healthy, wealthy and wise." Want to have a large checking account and a low LDL count? No need to read six library shelves' worth of self-help books. Just turn in at 8 and get up at 5. Simple, right?

So simple, in fact, that I've devised a new and astoundingly perspicacious set of aphorisms for life in the 21st century—short, astute summations that, if interpreted correctly, can get you to a satisfactory decision point in less time than it takes to slip on a cake of soap in the shower stall. Shall we, then? Oh, you bet we shall.

"Fool me once and shame on you. Fool me twice and shame on my parents, who apparently home-schooled me."

"Speed-dating the cable guy may render two hook-ups for one."

"Death is life's way of voting you off the island."

"Too much food does one no good... while a meal passed is no fun to look at."

"Never put off today what you can do tomorrow." No. Wait. That can't be right. "Always put off today what can't be done tomorrow." What the hell... OK, OK. Now I've got it. "Never try to say something clever about procrastination."

"If at first you don't succeed, run for Congress. If later you can't find anyone willing to engage in congress with you, it's probably because your constituents got tired of being screwed."

"A full belly makes a dull brain. That, of course, goes a long way toward explaining that reality TV show, *The Biggest Loser*."

"For the man who expects nothing... I have good news."

"Don't go to a doctor with every distemper, nor to a lawyer with every quarrel. I'd stay away from Mona Slutsky's cousin, too, or you'll wind up visiting both."

"Let he who scatters thorns not go barefoot. Washing the sand out of your swimsuit is probably a good idea, too."

"He who speaks much, most likely has little to say."

If only you'd known that a little earlier.

LOSING IT

New York transit officials dutifully collect and catalog more than 50,000 items a year lost on commuter trains, subways and buses, from wallets to smartphones. "We get false teeth almost every week," said William Bonner, supervisor of the New York City Transit Lost-and-Found Office.

            – Associated Press

They were staring at me from the seat across the aisle, gleaming with a dull plastic luster and rattling in tempo with the clattering tracks on the No. 6 line. What would they say, I wondered, had they actually been in someone's mouth?

I blinked and shook my head, dismissing the mental mist that had settled in after eight hours of turning sheets of semolina pasta into the perfectly trimmed stacks of linguini that, over the years, had secured for my employer, Buster's Noodles, the iconic reputation as New York's No. 1 choice for the temporary replacement of broken shoelaces. It had been a long day, and somewhere in the city an unsuspecting cook soon would find himself boiling strands of a paisley necktie that had gotten caught in the cutting machine and nearly cost me my life. From then on, I vowed, I would limit my fashion statement to the half-Windsor instead of the more complicated full-Windsor knot – a style change guaranteed to gain me a precious second or two in the likelihood of another emergency.

Who had left them there? The teeth, I mean. The wad of chewed Wrigley's was mine. (Hey. They never put enough waste receptacles in these cars.) And under what circumstance had they been deposited? After all, you don't just casually misplace false teeth on the subway. No. There had to be a story behind this. Something touching. Something ironic. Something... exotically romantic. Sure. That was it. Two people were Frenching and one of them accidentally inhaled the other's dentures. A coughing spasm ensued and these babies got sprayed across the seat.

Mmmm... probably not. That kind of encounter would've made the front page of the *Post*, and all I see here is a headline about some hooker operating out of a ficus plant in the lobby at Merrill Lynch.

OK. So if not romance, then what? Laughter? Wait a minute. Not bad. Not bad at all. We may be getting somewhere here. Let's see. Two guys heading downtown... to the Financial District, most likely. (Those choppers don't come cheap.) One decides to burn a few minutes by telling a corker – a real gut-wrencher – and the other laughs so hard he sends his uppers and lowers into orbit. They hit an innocent passerby, and to avoid a lawsuit the owner and his banker buddy make a quick exit, leaving the deadly projectile behind.

Say. That could work, you know? Good plot. Believable characters. Requisite mayhem. It all comes together... except maybe for that huge, unanswered question the audience is left with. I mean, now we have to know what the joke was, right? What kind of punch line is explosive enough to overcome the adhesive power of Fixodent®?

Nah. Not good enough. There has to be a better, more satisfying explanation than that. Something worthy of, say, an O. Henry, that iconic chronicler of New York tales. Yeah. There you go. Some young wife who loves to watch the soaps pawns her TV so she can buy a pot roast for her husband, who trades his false teeth so he can surprise her with a boxed DVD set of *The Guiding Light*.

The guy dies of a broken heart before the deal or the dentures get sealed, and in the confusion of EMTs and hospital gurneys, the fake chops get left behind. Beautiful! What a story! Where's Spielberg when you need him?

On the No. 4 train, I'm guessing. Staring in wonderment at a ficus plant.

A PROGNOSTIC PAUSE

Please. Stop with the e-mails.

If that sounds a little harsh, I don't mean it to be. Really. I'm not altogether unappreciative, and on a certain level, well... they're flattering, of course. I mean, not everybody receives daily entreaties from the organizers of the World Economic Forum to please, P-L-E-A-S-E show up at their event.

Oh, sure. All manner of plutocrats and politicians and celebrities from around the globe just kind of materialize, uninvited. (I hear Goldie Hawn and Benjamin Netanyahu will be making an appearance this year. No word yet from Sting.) Hey. How can they afford not to? Camera density – the number of Canons and Leicas per cubic media – is expected to be at an all-time high. So if you're a Katie Couric, for instance, and you're a no-show, well then... you quite literally have no show.

But I repeat. I won't be traveling to Davos this year. I have a dentist appointment.

Instead, I have sent ahead for consideration by world leaders a comprehensive collection of musings on a variety of topics I'm quite certain should cause a stir. That doesn't happen very much, by the way. Stir-causing, I mean. Even *USA Today* was underwhelmed by the anticipated so-what-ness of the event, citing in one of its columns the chief economist at IHS, a global consultancy, who acknowledged that "top-level political leadership give their speeches, but usually they don't tell you anything you don't already know."

Well, my friends, that changes – right here and right now – beginning with this revelation about...

Big Business

Unfortunately, the only things that get smaller about big business are the chief executive minds that run it.

Despite a galactic assortment of historical data loudly exhorting against the long-term success of large-scale mergers and acquisitions, an ungodly conjoining of already bulging businesses into hypertensive corporate behemoths will continue apace – all under the repeatedly disproven guise that two companies in the red equal one in the black.

Apparently, all it takes to rise to a gaspingly overpaid corporate leadership level is a demonstrated ineptitude in math and history.

Education

Aha! Now we understand why U.S. math and history test scores continue to compare abysmally with results in countries like, oh, I don't know... East Timor. Obviously, every fourth-grader in America has set his sights on being a senior business executive.

Economics

Let me be economical here. (Seems fitting, doesn't it?) The poor get poorer and the rich get richer. That is, until the 85 wealthiest men and women in the world make the ultra-arrogant mistake of actually accepting an invitation to a picnic being thrown by the 3.2 billion people on the planet who, believe it or not, as a group own less than they do. Somewhere near the hot dog grill they are essentially subsumed by the penniless masses and their bodies are never found. The authorities are called in to investigate, but honestly, how many interrogations can you reasonably expect to conduct? In 2051, the case goes cold.

Politics

Syrian President Bashar al-Assad finally sees the writing on the wall (You'd think that wouldn't be so hard for a bona fide eye doctor, wouldn't you?) and abdicates. Meanwhile, the Congressional logjam in Washington, D.C., is broken when, in an alcohol-induced fit of nostalgia at his improbable rise to power as the son of a Midwestern barkeep, Speaker of the House John Boehner drowns in his own tears.

Oh, and I almost forgot. Russian President Vladimir Putin succumbs to frostbite when he removes his shirt once too often at the Winter Olympics. The *New York Times* calls it "a chilling example of pectoral hubris," while across town the *Daily News* headline reads: **Putin Pecs? Permafrost, Pal**.

Technology

An unlikely successor to Steve Jobs is found when, following a coffee spill at an Apple board meeting, a janitor is overhead asking a senior technologist whether it would be possible to put a small windshield wiper on his iPhone.

Space and Aeronautics

NASA scientists are baffled when the Mars rover Curiosity inadvertently rolls over an empty pack of Lucky Strike cigarettes. Meanwhile, back on Earth, physicists' excitement over the discovery of Another World in Schenectady, N.Y., is dampened when it turns out to be the name of a local porn shop.

Culture

Lastly, the *New Yorker* finally agrees to publish a piece by this writer, but only after being presented with a JPEG featuring the magazine's humor editor committing uninhibited plagiarism with two ladies from a Las Vegas literary circle.

Hey. I'll take any advantage I can get.

GAME OF THRONES

Well, this explains everything.

All right, so maybe that's a tad too expansive. It does explain a couple of things, though, and these days if you can manage to get a sensible explanation for anything – especially anything Congressional – you're either channeling Christopher Hitchens or chugging Jack Daniel's.®

Since Hitchens himself would sneer at the idea of messages from the Great Beyond, I'm betting it's the bourbon. Not coincidentally, my odds in arriving at that conclusion were greatly improved by the fact that your family room floor appears to be strewn with empty liquor bottles.

But the family room isn't where I'd like us to be. Instead, let's go to the bathroom, shall we, where *USA Today* reports that adults aged 30-70 spend about an hour a day multi-tasking. Their primary task is self-evident, I'm sure, so we don't need to go there – pun fully and functionally intended. More revealing, I think, are the secondary activities noted in one of the newspaper's illuminating Snapshot graphics.

As documented by market researchers Yankelovich Partners, a full 53 percent of bowl-bound American adults spend their time reading. Following close behind (OK, that pun just crept up on me, but I'm leaving it in), 47 percent while away the hour in deep thought. Another 33 percent occupy themselves by chatting on the phone.

Now... I don't know about you, but for me, those results are interesting on a couple of levels. First, when you add up all the numbers, the total comes to 133 percent. It took a while for me to figure it out, but if you leave your inhibitions at the door, the answer is obvious: At least a third of the time, survey respondents had someone else in the bathroom with them. Not making any judgments here, OK? Just saying...

Second, if you're talking to people on your smart phone, how do you keep them – and how do they keep you – from overhearing what, in scientific terms, might be called extraneous alimentary audio? You know. Potentially embarrassing sound waves generated by the mildly explosive goings-on that usually occur in small rooms paved with reverberatory tiles. Is there an app for that kind of thing? Some noise-cancellation technology made specifically for that purpose?

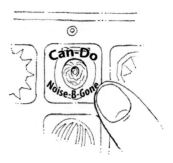

If there isn't, then I want to make something perfectly clear to the chief audio technologist at Bose Inc. who, based on the survey results, is undoubtedly reading this in his own executive washroom and simultaneously emailing a link to R&D. Everything in this provocative little essay is copyrighted, do you hear me?

In fact, just to make sure you do, I'm giving you a phone call right now.

Think about that.

BRUSH WITH FAME

"Curious," I muttered to myself, having completed a flagrantly illicit flip through the pages of the latest *AARP Bulletin*. It's a newspaper for retired persons, after all, and still I incessantly labor, recording my taxable hours on a kitchen time clock provided by my agelessly beautiful bride. Punch it, I believe were her exact words. Or get punched.

The source of my intrigue was an article titled "Great Hoaxes of the Last 50 years"– just one in an endless supply of factoids offered by the editors as a clever means of easing readers into the universally unpalatable idea of death. "So what if you're losing a little bladder control," they seem to be suggesting. "Don't get so upset. Everyone gets older. Nothing's exempt. Look. There's even a hoax here that's half a century old." Sort of leaves you suspecting the hoax story itself is a bit of a hoax, doesn't it?

Anyway, it wasn't the magazine's inept attempt at downplaying my lumbago that piqued my curiosity. It was one of the featured frauds. "In February 1964," the writer revealed, "a previously unknown French artist, Pierre Brassau, earned lavish praise when his work was exhibited at a Swedish art show. 'Pierre is an artist who performs with the delicacy of a ballet dancer,' one critic said. A lone reviewer said the works could have been painted by an ape. He was right. Pierre Brassau was an alias for Peter, a 4-year-old chimpanzee."

What else, I wondered, could we get monkeys to do in a passably human fashion? Are there other occupations, the requirements of which are minimal enough, that simians might make suitable practitioners? Are there, in fact, chimpanzees filling those roles right now, earning misguided praise from humans who wouldn't know a rhesus from a Rembrandt? The answer, as I'm sure you have perspicaciously guessed, is an astonishing 'Yes.' I mean, come on. How much fun would 'No' have been? There wasn't a farcical chance in hell that that was going to happen, right? For your consideration, then, I offer the following.

Congressional Representatives: Have you actually seen one in anything other than a televised environment? That has to be a tip-off right there, doesn't it? And what about the nonsensical yammering that passes for speech when the worst of these yahoos open their mouths for something besides breathing? Cripes, people. Cheetah carried on a more intelligent conversation with Johnny Weissmuller.

Add to that the indiscriminate flinging of verbal feces at political opponents, and I think we have enough to insist on some fairly stringent DNA testing.

Investment Bankers: This I'm not making up. A couple of years ago researchers at two prestigious universities wondered whether capuchin monkeys with a knack for trading tokens for food would know a bargain when they saw one, so they conducted a little experiment. They gave the monkeys 12 tokens and offered two capuchin favorites for 'sale' – apples and Jell-O cubes. Unsurprisingly, the furry financiers spent half their money on the Granny Smiths and half on the gelatin.

The next day the apples were available at the same exchange rate, but the Jell-O salesman engaged in a bit of volume discounting and offered two cubes for the price of one. Bingo. There was a run on the jiggly stuff. The upshot, concluded the researchers, is that a monkey's market sense is remarkably similar to a human's.

Certainly goes a long way toward explaining the Great Recession, doesn't it? Perhaps some follow-up research is in order. I, for one, would be very interested in tracking the bulk shipment of bananas to executive suites at Merrill Lynch.

Chatroom Technicians: Especially the ones working for Internet service providers. It's obvious, isn't it, that all the instant message replies to your simple and intelligently outlined inquiries about cell phone malfunctions are being randomly punched out by a room full of bonobo chimps. How else are we supposed to explain chat threads that pretty much all look like this:

- Hi. I can't get my iPhone to link with my household Wi-Fi. Can you help?

- Dwnld app 'n synch uzing pprclipz 'n bubgum (Errrp!)

- Say what?

- µ¶$¥àáβ3̌grapesgoodφℂ⅃ͻτογ☼₄⅜⑲↥◇wheremolly??

Auto Mechanics: Listen. There's a reason your car comes back to you with an expensive ailment that's altogether different from the one you brought in to get fixed. If that doesn't convince you, ask yourself why you're never allowed into the part of the garage where your Toyota's getting all better. Is it really a matter of safety... or does it have to do with the bad press that can come from professionally uncertified simians dueling it out with pneumatic lug nut wrenches? Seriously. I'm beginning to wonder whether all those stuttering explosive sounds even have anything to do with pneumatic lug nut wrenches.

Humorists: Really? You need to ask?

In(ad)vertently Yours

Brands including Barbie, iPod, Mug Root Beer and Life Savers showed up on standardized English tests more than a million New York students in grades 3-8 took, leading to speculation it was some form of product placement advertising.

— Associated Press

Please leave your pencils on the desk next to your achievement tests until I tell you to begin. Silvio, that means you. Yes, I saw what you did. Take it out of Eric's ear and put it back on your desk. No, you cannot have another one. Well, you should have thought about that before you decided today was the day to jump-start your career as an otolaryngologist. Oh, stop whining. It'll probably fall off when you use the eraser. Given the ubiquitous appearance of the letter "F" on your last report card, I'm guessing you'll be using that part of your pencil a lot. What? No. Sorry. I'm not allowed to tell you what "ubiquitous" means. Because it's one of the questions on the test, that's why. No. I don't know exactly how many questions there are. Let's just say they're everywhere.

Now... the doors are closing and the perimeter is being patrolled by monitors, so from this point on no one will be permitted to leave the room until their test is completed. No, not even for a drink of water, Melissa. Well, perhaps you should have stopped at our shiny soda machine on the way in and quenched your thirst with a delicious Benson's Blackberry Fizz. Maybe next time you'll think ahead.

All right, children. The test is about to start. Please pick up your pencils and begin... NOW!

There are two Twinkies in a package, and Geraldo has four packages. He gives one package to Susie and eats three of the delicious crème-filled sponge cakes for dessert. How many individual Twinkies does he have left? Bonus question: How many tablespoons of Phillips' Milk of Magnesia does Geraldo's mother have to give him to clear his intestinal blockage?

Fill in the blank: Skippy Peanut Butter is to Welch's Grape Jelly as Boar's Head _____ is to Kraft Swiss Cheese. Boy, you must be getting pretty hungry by now. Don't you wish you had a handful of Lay's Potato Chips to go with either one of those mouth-watering sandwich combos?

Which of these commenced in 1847? **a.** The Reese Peace Treaty, or **b.** a treat of Reese's Pieces.

A Ford Fusion gets an impressive 38 miles per gallon while a Chevy Malibu clocks in at a disappointing 27 mpg. If gas at her local Cumberland Farms is $3.90 a gallon, how much money will Sally save by driving 100 miles in the Ford instead of the Chevy? Bonus question: How much gas will she get if she snarfs down six of Cumby's irresistible Mac 'n Cheese Bites along the way?

Which of these is the proper spelling of a world-famous department store? **a.** Macy's **b.** Macy's **c.** Macy's **d.** They all are.

Permafrost is **a.** frozen subsoil in an arctic region, or **b.** an exciting new hair style available exclusively at Frank's Fancy Follicles. Stop in for a free manicure!

TIME'S UP! Put your Dixon Ticonderoga No. 2 pencils down and pass your tests forward. That's right. All the way up front. Good. Thank you. Your buses are waiting at the main entrance. Hurry along now. Yes, Silvio? Is there something you need? Oh, my. For me? A lip-smacking Granny Smith from Herb's Orchard-Fresh Fruits, you say.... Where It's Never Wrong to be Ripe.™

DAVID, REIMAGINED

Romania's Ministry of Culture has demanded that the breasts on a statue of a former prime minister's wife be resculpted because they're too big. Pompiliu Ciolacu, head of the Gorj County Culture Department, said "Artistically, it's exaggerated, and that means that aesthetically it doesn't resemble the real image of the person." The complaint was rejected by the artist, who is refusing to make the breasts smaller.

— Orange News (UK)

"Mr. Michelangelo?"

"Yes? (laying down his chisel) Do I know you?"

"I suppose you could say that. I, um... I'm the intern you hired to model your statue. You know... David?"

"Ah, yes. Of course. How are you?"

"Oh, fine, I guess. I'm posing for Leonardo now, although he hasn't actually started the piece yet. Hmm. Now that I think of it, he hasn't even ordered the marble. That's a little disconcerting, isn't it..."

"How may I help you?"

"Oh, right. Well, I was hoping I could talk to you about the David."

"One of my more critically acclaimed works, I'm pleased to say. I wasn't sure at first, but I'm told the response has been overwhelmingly favorable. Did you hear? They're moving it to the public square, just outside the government center at the Palazzo della Signoria. (smiling now) What a break, huh? Every schmuck paying a parking ticket in downtown Florence is gonna run into that baby."

"Yes, well... that's, um, one of my concerns."

(hint of indignation) "What do you mean?"

"No, listen... I agree with what everybody else is saying. It's an artistic tour de force, you know? The drawn brow, the tense neck. The sense of motion. And my lord, those spring-loaded quads. They must have cost me about a million deep-knee bends. Really. It's absolutely stunning."

"So what's the problem?"

"Well, there's just one little thing. And I mean that literally."

"I don't understand."

"Let's call it... the frontispiece, shall we? It's a tad small, don't you think?"

"Oh, my God. You're kidding, right?"

"Come on, Mike. You gotta agree – it really doesn't do me justice. I mean, sure, your studio can get pretty chilly in the evening, but even taking that into account..."

"Look. I sculpt what I feel. Wait. That didn't come out the way I planned. I sculpt what I see. And what I saw was in perfect proportion to the rest of the body."

"Oh, sure. This from the guy who manages to displace 15 liters every time he wades into Lake Como!"

"It's true. (pensively) There generally is some minor flooding..."

"I'm just sayin..."

"All right, all right. But I still don't get why it's so important."

"Really? This somehow manages to escape you? Geez, Mike. I'm still in circulation here, you know? I'm out there every Friday night trying to scrape up dates, and something like this doesn't exactly make for effective advertising, if you know what I mean."

"I guess. But what am I supposed to do about it now? The thing is finished, dude. Complete. I can't go back and just reattach what I've already chiseled off. I mean, yeah, I'm good, but..."

"Look. I know I'm asking a lot, but maybe if you took a little more off the hips and the pelvic region, everything else would look bigger by comparison. What do you think?"

"Merde. (sighing) I am such a pushover. OK, fine. Let me see what I can do. Just gimme a few days to come up with something, will ya?"

"Sure. Sure. And thanks, Mike. Thanks a lot."

[*Later that night, under cover of darkness*]

(Michelangelo, muttering to himself sarcastically) "Geez, Mike. It doesn't exactly make for effective advertising, does it? Man. The things I do to appease my adoring public. All right. Let's see. Maybe I can shave a little off the lower belly. Yeah. This looks like a good spot. Relatively few fracture lines. Just a little tap right here and... oops."

UNINDICTABLE, THAT'S WHAT YOU ARE...

"He promises to just smoke pot as mayor, not crack." That's one of three outrageous campaign slogans that popped up all around Toronto, spoofing the bad behavior of Canada's favorite substance-abusing incumbent mayor Rob Ford. Although Ford has admitted smoking crack, driving drunk and urinating in public, he has refused calls to step down, even after being stripped of many of his powers by the city council.

– nbcnews.com

All right. So where your average exasperated constituent sees yet another cringe-worthy development in the continuing degeneration of political gamesmanship, I see hope. I see a brighter day. I see the distinct possibility of... an endgame.

How, you say? Well, now I'm puzzled. Why would you say that? Unless, of course, you're a member of one of the great Native American tribes of the sprawling Midwest, say... oh, I don't know... Lakota Sioux. On second thought, please don't say Lakota Sioux, because that will just take us farther off track. How do these things happen, anyway? No, wait. I know exactly how. It's because I used the word "how" instead of "why." Well, that's not going to happen anymore, I promise. No way, no how.

Now... where were we. Oh, yes. Why, you say? Why do I see the distinct possibility of an endgame? Because I'm one of the very few people on the planet familiar with an abstract concept called the Black Hole Theory of Political Campaign Ads, which goes something like this: Succumbing to the weight of their own heavy-handed stupidity, all political ads – as well as the candidates behind them – sink to their lowest gravitational level, finally slipping over their own event horizons to disappear into absurdity.

Listen. This is a simple political application of relativistic physics. You know. $E=MC^2$. The more these ad campaigns gain energy, the less matter they make, until ultimately they dematerialize.

Eyes still rolling? OK. First I'm going to presume your name isn't Groucho, and second I'm going to suggest we use a current example to see how it all works. Let's see. Just what example might that be?

Yeah, right. Like you didn't know where this was going.

Ford Ad No. 1 (Candidate announces re-election bid)

Yup. I smoked. I drank. I relieved myself on a fire hydrant in downtown Toronto and got away with it, so I'm running again. Christ, who wouldn't? This is one sweet gig.

Opposition Ad No. 1

Listen. My bladder has a mind of its own, so when it comes to public urination, I'm not making any promises. But I will say this: As mayor, you have my word that I won't smoke crack – just pot.

Ford Ad No. 2

All right, all right. Apparently this stuff matters to you people, so I'll do the other guy one better and promise to use the men's room... whenever possible. Geez. I had no idea the voting public could be so touchy.

Opposition Ad No. 2

Hmm. I see Ford vowed to keep the streets dry. Damn tricky of him. OK, so I'll match that AND swear off the drinking. Yeah, I know. There goes the multi-million-dollar campaign contribution from Labatt's, but what are you gonna do?

Ford Ad No. 3

What? No drinking! Hell, I don't know if I want this job anymore. All right, all right. No drinking AND no unrestrained elimination. That can't be too bad, right? I mean, now that I'm giving up one, maybe I won't need the other. Still... public service sure ain't what it used to be.

Opposition Ad No. 3

Well, I guess I don't have any choice, do I. No drinking, no public urination AND no drugs. Just responsible government service, top to bottom.

Ford Ad No. 4

I'm out.

Skin in the Game

Discovery Channel is offering a sneak peek of a new Naked
and Afraid *season that features a single man and woman
who've never met, in new, exotic locations.* TLC's Buying
Naked *focuses on a real estate agent who works in Florida
nudist communities. And VH1 unveils* Dating Naked, *putting
all the mystery that's usually saved for later and in the dark
on display from the first moment these couples meet.*

— USA Today

Apparently, the fall lineup will be featuring reality TV programs of a different strip.

Stripe. Sorry. I mean stripe.

And no one's particularly surprised, are they? With audiences becoming increasingly inured to well-endowed but mostly clothed bachelors, bachelorettes and *Big Brother* bed buddies, broadcast executives are throwing down the gauntlet... along with halter tops and underpants and any other bothersome piece of fabric that threatens to get between the camera lens and better Nielsen ratings. Not since 1953, when Lady Godiva made an unexpected appearance at a séance in Bayonne, N.J., has anyone channeled so much nudity.

All of which kind of begs the question: How long before we're presented with yet another innovative reality TV program, one that features (yes... you heard it here first) naked people watching naked reality TV shows? Happily, not long at all.

What's On Tonight? And Let's Take Everything Off To Watch It. (The pilot)

Phil: Cripes, is it cold in here or what? Throw me that coverlet, will you, Holly?

Holly: Sorry, Phil. The contract specifically prohibits obscuring any part of our naked forms. The closest you're getting to an Afghan tonight is the Evening News.

Phil: Oh, yeah. I forgot. Any restrictions on adjusting the thermostat?

Holly: Well, I don't see any...

Phil: Good. Just reach over and turn that up a bit for me. Thanks. That should be good for the O'Reillys, too. Frank's got some circulation problems. They're coming over tonight, right?

Holly: Are you kidding? Shirley must have dropped $75 at the tanning salon this afternoon. They'll be here. (doorbell rings) That's probably them now.

Phil: I'll get it. Frank! Shirley! How are you? Here... let me take your coats. And your shirts. And your pants. Wow! Looking good, Shirl. Just that one little tan line...

Shirl: Oh, I know. It's silly, isn't it? They positively insist on having you wear a little something down there. Health laws, or hygiene, or something like that.

Frank: (shivering) Geez, Phil. You got the air conditioning on? My toes are turning blue.

Holly: (suddenly walking into frame) Not to mention one or two other extremities. Ha, ha, ha! What can I get you guys?

Shirl: A nice glass of pinot grigio would be good.

Frank: Martini. Straight up.

Phil: Easy, Frank. We've got network stipulations against anything straight up.

Frank: (winking) I don't know, buddy. With these two gorgeous babes joining us on the couch, I'm thinking we may be in for a little breach of contract tonight.

Phil: You dog, you.

Shirl: So... what are we watching this evening? I mean besides the regression of two grown-ups into college frat boys.

Phil: Good lineup. You're gonna like this. First we're tuning into the Nude News...

Shirl: (interrupting) Does it look like Scott Pelley's been working out a little more than usual? I mean, my God. We may need to upgrade to a 70-inch screen just to accommodate those pecs.

Phil: ... then straight into Law and Order: Naked Aggression.

Frank: Best cop show on television. I love the look of confusion on their faces when they try to holster their weapons.

Phil: OK, then. Let me find the remote and... (doorbell rings again)

Holly: Can you get that, Phil? I'm still working on the drinks. It's probably the pizza guy.

Phil: Sure. Wait a minute... I don't have any money.

Holly: What!?

Frank: Don't look at me...

Phil: Um, Shirl. You don't happen to have a few bucks, do you?

Shirl: Do I look like I have any cash on me?

Phil: Damn. Well, that's that. No dinner.

Holly: Oh, no!

Phil: Yeah. I guess we might as well call it a night.

Shirl: But why?

Phil: Focus groups. Viewers say the only reason they come back every week is to see Frank spilling something hot on himself.

Holly: No steaming mozzarella, no show. See? They're starting to roll the credits already.

Phil: Listen. Let's all just get dressed and play strip poker. Maybe we can still save this...

(Music up. Fade to commercial.)

BEAN THERE

A chef has been forced to quit his job because of an uncontrollable fear of baked beans. The man left his job as a pub chef because he felt faint every time he saw the food. [He] believes his rare fear – technically known as leguminophobia – was a result of his brothers throwing beans at him as a child. [The ex-chef], who now works as a window cleaner, said he can't even go near beans, which he calls 'orange devils.'

– Metro.co.uk

What will it take, I ask you, to finally get CBS News interested in my gastroenterological aversion to Brussels sprouts? I mean, come on. Seems like they've got plenty of time to fill, doesn't it? *48 Hours. 60 Minutes.* They couldn't take 5 or 10 of 'em to videotape me trying to choke down one of these babies? That would be hours, by the way. Not minutes.

Baked beans? Sure. That'll get you some airtime. An in-depth examination of the haunting effects of leguminophobia on the human psyche? No problem. That's most likely Leslie Stahl at the front door right now.

But the life-saving extraction of a little green bowling ball from a constricted esophagus using a 12-horsepower Wet-Dry Vac and the Jaws of Life? From the national news desk, a big fat no. Just doesn't have what it takes to keep today's TV audience from fishing out the floss to have yet another go at that nagging piece of pork lodged somewhere between the second and third molars.

It's discouraging, you know? Here you have someone with a bona fide fear of a food product – *petit cabbage pètrification*, I think they call it – and I can't get anyone to pay attention. Not even the specialists. And I've seen plenty of them, mister, including an upstate vegetable farmer who escorted me off his property after misinterpreting an offhand comment about fertile bottomland as an affront to his wife. He was wrong, of course. I know fallow acreage when I see it.

And while the medical community seems determined to attribute my affliction to a rare peristaltic deficiency, I'm not swallowing it. This goes much deeper. Psychologically, I mean. It wouldn't surprise me, for instance, to discover that my current phobia traces all the way back to the summer of '55, when my sisters surreptitiously dropped half a dozen sprouts into my bathing suit, inciting panic at the South Street natatorium as, one by one, they floated out of my pants and bobbed to the surface.

"But what about the health benefits," you ask. "Surely you understand that the fiber-related components in a cruciferous vegetable like Brussels sprouts do a superb job of binding with bile acids and lowering your cholesterol." Well, I do now, sport. And thanks so much for sharing. What is it about the words "uncontrollable fear" that you don't understand? Now I have this indelible image of a two-inch sphere squeezing its way through one of my arteries, like a mouse working its way through a snake's digestive tract. Wait a minute. Did you hear that? There it is again. Like something just plopped into my right ventricle...

Well, that's it. If they aren't going to profile me on the Evening News, then I'm switching channels and taking an extended vacation. Someplace in Europe, maybe.

I hear Belgium is nice.

Nothing Doing

Houston Oasis is one of a growing number of so-called atheist churches in the U.S. designed to appeal to those who long for the rituals of old-time religion but have lost faith in its doctrines. The rise of atheist churches is part of a growing willingness by many atheists to adopt secular versions of religious practices.

— Time

Welcome, friends, on this randomly beautiful Sunday, to the Church of the Immaculate Dissension. There's plenty of room up here, so don't be afraid to join us in the front pews. That's right, step forward. And please... don't be concerned about the Widow Bungfelder. She suffers from a bona fide medical condition called Tourette's syndrome, and those sudden outbursts have nothing whatever to do with demonic possession. Although you do have to wonder where she picked up all those words.

As you find your way to your seats, you might want to help yourselves to some of that fluorinated dihydrogen monoxide flowing from the porcelain wall fonts provided by the Municipal Water Department. You'll find it to be a blessing on this unseasonably hot day – a phenomenon we all know is scientifically proven to be caused by nothing more than a naturally occurring inversion in the jet stream.

We'll begin with a reading from the Book of Allen. (Ahem) Sayeth the prophet Woody: "How can I believe in God when just last week I got my tongue caught in the roller of an electric typewriter? If only God would give me some clear sign! Like making a large deposit in my name at a Swiss bank."

Amen.

Our sermon this week is derived from a series of musings by the renowned cosmologist Lawrence Krauss, haphazardly cherry-picked from his highly regarded book, *A Universe From Nothing*. The entirety of our observable cosmos, he writes, "can start out as a microscopically small region of space, which can be essentially empty, and still grow to enormous scales." Just how seriously can we take such an assertion? Well, I'm not ruling out the possibility that there may be one in my clothes hamper. How else do you explain the fact that two socks go in and only one comes out?

All of that can transpire without losing a drop of energy, Krauss contends, leaving behind enough matter and radiation to account for everything we see today. The upshot, he concludes, is that "something" can indeed come from nothing – all without the need for divine guidance. Certainly I can attest to the fact that, in preparing today's homily, the only guidance I required were directions to the church sacristy, where, it turns out, we store huge amounts of communion sherry.

What we are left with, then, is a world where the price of everything that has come into existence since the beginning of time is essentially nothing... which means my mortgage company has been screwing me every month for the past 23 years. Additionally, with God out of the picture, there's no logical place for heaven. And in the absence of heaven, there obviously is no hell to go to, either... despite Mrs. Bungfelder's continual insistence that we do so.

Amen.

That brings us to the collection segment of our service. If the segue seems ironic, it's because the total from last week's offertory was – you guessed it – nothing. We're hoping to do better this time by reminding everyone that you're supposed to pass the basket on... not pass on the basket.

Lastly, I'm pleased to note that, through the generosity of two longtime parishioners, refreshments will be served following today's service. The lemonade has been made available by Mrs. Gertrude Boniface in memory of her deceased pug-nosed boxer, Sourpuss, and dessert has been provided by Mrs. Bungfelder who, for those of you in the back who might have missed it, encourages us to eat it, you goddamn asshole shitheads.

Amen.

HEAR YE, HEAR YE

Men's ears, it turns out, grow bigger as they get older. I know this is because I overheard two women talking about it in Grand Central Station. I was two blocks away on Madison Avenue at the time. In a cab. Stopped next to a guy using a jackhammer.

The topic apparently gained some currency recently in the *Register*, a British newspaper, after former Member of Parliament-turned columnist Matthew Parris caused a bit of a flap (That seems like a term appropriate to the discussion, doesn't it?) by publicly fretting about the size of the cartilaginous satellite dishes attached to his own noggin. "They started quite big," he confessed, "and now it's become embarrassing. Are there any pills you can take to shrink them? Never mind penis enlargement. I'm looking for ear reduction."

His predicament is worthy of consideration, of course, although I don't know how much sympathy he expects to buy with such a sensational mix of metaphors. Certainly if someone asked yours truly to logically associate the subjects of male genitalia and big ears, about the only response I could come up with is that I seem to be listening to myself an awful lot lately.

Paradoxically, the idea of men's ears growing longer as they age is not altogether, um, unheard of. The *Register*, in fact, went so far as to note a 1995 issue of the *British Medical Journal*, in which a study of 206 middle-aged patients showed that "as we get older, our ears get bigger" (on average by 0.22mm a year). I'm sorry, what? You didn't hear that? I see. Well, obviously your ears aren't large enough... which means you're probably a hell of a lot younger than the rest of us.

As you might suspect, my own ears have no particular claim to immunity when it comes to the ravages of time. As a matter of fact, I'm standing on them right now. And yes, that most assuredly can have a limiting effect on personal mobility, which is why I quite often resort to tucking them into my pants pockets. It's a solution I would not hesitate to recommend to Mr. Parris, by the way, especially given what seems to be a desire to simultaneously reduce the apparent size of his ears and mislead people into thinking his pocket rocket may be larger than it actually is.

All of that would amount to small change, though, if, as a disadvantaged group, we could just get our ears out of the way and address the lucrative business opportunity standing right in front of us. Wait. What was that? Is everyone OK? Oh, my stars and comets. Could someone please give him a hand with those things? That's right. Move him away from the open window. A little breeze and those babies can turn lethal. Good. Now somebody help the lady to her feet.

Let's see... where were we? Oh, yes. That lucrative business opportunity. Well, here it is: designer clothing for the cartilaginously challenged. Garments and apparel creatively fabricated to accommodate and strategically de-emphasize out-of-control ears. Shirts with over-sized collars and hidden compartments in which to tuck away awkward flaps and folds. Hidden shoulder holsters to keep dangerously long lobes out of earshot. Pants with sewn-in channels to direct the most serious mutations into specially designed dress socks.

A potential goldmine, I'm sure you'll agree, but, yes – perhaps it is a bit early to be cashing our checks. There are angel investors to identify. Venture capitalists to convince. We just need to get out there and bang the drums. But before we do, let's take an inspirational moment to realize just how far we've already come, shall we?

Think about it, my friends. Together, we have risen to stand against our harshest critics – theatergoers in constant complaint that we're blocking their view; tennis fans in tournament galleries temporarily blinded when we turn our heads too fast. We have joined to face our aural adversities with courage and determination, and let nothing stand in our way.

We are steadfast in our purpose and resolute in our will.

We are, in a word... unflappable.

IN THE BLACK

Scientists have created the 'new black,' and it's so dark it's like gazing into a black hole. The material, called Vantablack, absorbs all but 0.035 percent of visual light. It is so dark that the human eye cannot understand what it is seeing because all shapes and contours are hidden. If it was used to make one of Coco Chanel's little black dresses, the wearer's head and limbs would appear to float around a frock-shaped hole.

– Metro.co.uk

"*Señor Zorro*, a package awaits you in the *vestíbulo*. Overnight, I think."

"Ah yes, Bernardo. Probably my new costume. I was in Geraldo's Haberdashery the other day, where Gerry himself fitted me with exquisite new raiments featuring the latest breakthrough in fabric for avenging swordsmen."

"What? Another outfit? Listen, Don Diego, with all due respect, these disguises don't come cheap. I mean, I'm talking some extensive *dinero* here. *Dio mios*, your cape alone cost a small fortune. And the *sombrero cordobés*... Jesus. We had that on lay-away for six months."

"True, it was expensive, but I ask you to remember, Bernie. I am a Spanish nobleman, and attention to fashion must be paid.

Besides, there was a hole in my trousers where I missed the sash that time and stuck my rapier in my pants pocket."

"*Si, señor*. You came very close, as I remember, to riding side-saddle into the sunset."

"Lady Lolita (heh, heh) would have been sorely disappointed."

"And you, Don Diego de la Vega, would have been sorely disappendaged."

"This I do not like to think about, Bernardo. Here... let us examine my new duds."

"I'll open it. I'll open it. You're the nobleman and I'm the servant, remember? Oh, man... not again. Looks like you got screwed, Donny boy. There's nothing in here."

(sniggering) "Ah, my dear Bernardo. So you might think. But no. There are, indeed, items of men's apparel in this package. See? Here are my new slacks... (slipping into them)

"Gasp!"

"... and this is my elegant new blouse. See how it drapes so fluidly about my shapely pectorals?"

"My God, *Señor Zorro*! I see nothing but your floating noggin and two disembodied but finely manicured hands!"

"Yes, well... I stopped by the nail parlor, too. I know. I know. We could save a few *centavos* if I let you do them, but honestly, Bernie. Look at how these babies shine. I can see my pencil-thin moustache in them!"

"*Si.* Pencil-thin. Your moustache and your bank balance. (sigh). All right. All right. What else have you got in there? Gloves, I expect."

"But of course. See how splendidly they hide my, um...expensively manicured fingers. Hmm. I see now my miscalculation. (heh, heh) Maybe next time I come to Bernardo for a buffing, yes?"

"Let's get back to the costume, shall we? I don't see a hat or a mask."

"No, and neither will Sergeant Gonzales and his bumbling *compadres*. Those accouterments are, indeed, part of my new disguise (reaching into the box), and as I affix them to my fastidiously coiffed melon, you see the stunning result."

"*Dio mios, Señor Zorro.* You have completely disappeared!"

"*Si.* Neither you nor the authorities – nor even I – can see where I am. Now hand me my rapier so I may sheath it in my sash and rejoin the fight against injustice. Ow!"

"What? What happened?"

"It is nothing, Bernardo. A slight scratch. Help me to my horse, *por favor.* That is, if you can find me (heh, heh)."

(One week later, at the Mission of Our Lady of the Spanish Fly)

"A fitting service, don't you think, Bernardo? He was adored by so many – especially, it would seem, by attendants in men's fashion retail."

"*Si.* I will miss him. I wonder, my good Sergeant, would you mind very much recounting the details of his demise? I mean, given the special qualities of his costume, how was it that you managed to bring him down?"

"Let me tell you, my friend. It took some doing. For the longest time, all I could see was the flash of Spanish steel, you know? It was as if I was being attacked by a sword with a mind of its own. But just as I was weakening, I noticed something strange."

"*Que?*"

"Socks. Two dirty white socks – of the athletic variety, I believe – momentarily darting into view and vanishing again. The next time they appeared, I aimed in the middle and took a shot."

Color Me Incredulous

Sen. Ted Cruz, another potential GOP presidential candidate, is the subject of Ted Cruz Saves America, *a coloring book that depicts the Texan as a superhero.*

– USA Today

Yes. It's true. Given the obvious Crayola® connection, my first inclination was to wax poetic. I mean, who wouldn't? The idea of kindergarteners in West Texas smilingly scribbling Ted Cruz into the annals of American superhero-dom stirred something in me, you know? At first I thought it might be patriotism, but damned if it didn't turn out to be nausea, so the best I could do was wax emetic.

Really? Ted Cruz? The Canadian ex-pat who somehow managed to physically relocate to a new home in the Lone Star State while leaving his intellect in a Lonesome State back in Calgary? Am I missing something here? Besides Ted's modesty, I mean. What could possibly be behind such a stupefyingly obvious public relations stunt aimed at turning a do-nothing politician into Captain America?

Oh, wait. Of course. The P-R-E-S-I-D-E-N-C-Y. The Cruz Master is contemplating a run for the Oval Office in 2016, and this is his answer to the requisite historical biography routinely published these days by every candidate for head of state who wants to be taken seriously. Barack Obama had his *Dreams From My Father*. Hillary Clinton has her *Hard Choices*. Ted has his coloring book.

Listen. If I'm being too hard on the Ted-ster, just say so, OK? I've always had trouble staying inside the lines. Just pass me a fresh crayon and I'll see if I can do better. Oooo! Pink Sherbet! Somebody get me a spoon!

Actually, in this case, I'm thinking a shovel might be more in order, as well as another, more suitable hue. Something along the lines of, say, Voluminous Manure. Does Crayola make that one?

The irony, of course, is that there really is something deeply red, white and blue about Cruz' approach to grass-roots political mythology – the cheesy appeal to the lowest common denominator, the ascent of fiction over fact, the reduction of complicated issues to the cartoonish simplicity of **Wham!** and **Biff!** and **Pow!** We're Americans, damn it all, and it's in our DNA to love guys who save the day just by showing up in flashy, skin-tight costumes and standing there with their hands on their hips.

Whoa. Does anybody else suddenly feel like tuning in to *Dancing With the Stars*?

Anyway, I'm thinking the Cruz-er may be on to something here, so I've decided to inveigle my way into elementary school minds across the country by publishing my own coloring book. It's called *Dougie Wowser: Washington Watchdog and American Mac 'n' Cheese Master*.

On page 1, for instance, kids can see me using my X-ray vision to find out just how much corporate super PAC money Mitch McConnell has in his wallet. I'd recommend Laser Lime to add some pizzazz to the fireballs emanating from my eyeglasses. (Discriminating crayon connoisseurs will quickly discern I'm having a bit of trouble controlling my rays with pin-point accuracy. For those sophisticated Crayolers, I'd suggest Erotic Red to fill in the hearts on Sen. McConnell's boxer shorts.)

Four pages later you'll find me flying Massachusetts Senator and avowed Wall Street avenger Elizabeth Warren over the Washington Monument to get her to the Capitol on time to vote against a pro-banking bill. Yeah. I know. It looks like she's kicking and screaming. There was a little mix-up back at my Fortress of Lassitude and I misread the Congressional Calendar. Turns out the legislation was actually coming up the next day. You can use your Blankety-blank Blue to cover up all those !#%&?$#! signs.

And yes, that's me on page 12, delivering a freight car-full of Jimmy Dean Smoked Bacon Mac & Cheese® to hungry fourth-graders at an under-funded elementary school in D.C. Jesus that stuff is good. It's kinda like my kryptonite, you know? I can't get near it without going all weak in the knees, so I'll need you kids to use your Pec-Power flesh-colored crayons to build up my chest muscles a tad. That's right. Just to balance out that little paunch I've got going.

Thanks. And keep coloring. By the time you get to that twenty-dollar bill on the last page, you should be damn close to counterfeit quality.

IF NOT ME, THEN WHO?

I'm ashamed to admit it, but the other day I was Googling myself. No, not that kind. The kind without lubricants. What's wrong with you people anyway?

Turns out there's a Who's Who of Doug Millers out there without any one of them actually being me. Body-builders. Economists. Psychologists. Politicians. Musicians. Lawyers. Insurance agents. Even a soccer coach. If maintaining a squeaky clean Facebook page could somehow have earned him time off for good behavior, I'm convinced I eventually would have turned up some convict named Doug doing time for wearing underwear with holes in it. All I can say is, they'll never pin that wrap on me.

I am guilty, however, of concluding that – in a strange and wondrous, and perhaps even sickening way – all those exceptional people are, in fact, me. I mean,

think about it. Body-builder? I lift and press overstuffed 30-gallon kitchen trash bags twice a day. Economist? Listen. The regional business engine would run out of gas if it weren't for my weekly consultation with the proprietor of the local wine warehouse. Psychologist? Come on. You think it doesn't take one deep and insightful understanding of the human psyche to come to the realization that all of it – every last damn thing – is my fault?

Needless to say, I am in some ridiculous way every one of those other specialists, too. Which led to this epiphany: Absolute strangers could probably learn a little something from a guy whose Internet presence is both non-existent and ubiquitous at the same time, don't you think? Of course you do. I know, because there's a clairvoyant Doug floating around out there, too.

Hence my hastiness in piecing together a collection of guiding-light epigrams from all who are me – an assemblage of wisdom and cosmic insight that, at least for the first edition, I'm calling Miller's Familiar Quotations. Don't be surprised if you've never heard of them.

On Body-building

They're called six-pack abs for a reason. If a mysterious seventh bulge should suddenly appear, you went too far and gave yourself a hernia.

On the Body Politic

Once, a long time ago, lawmakers stood on soapboxes. I'm beginning to think none of them even washes anymore.

On Psychology

Don't even think about it. I'm serious. You'll drive yourself crazy.

On Sex

In these matters, it's generally best not to offer an exposition. Unless, of course, you've had the good fortune to experience a triple-X position – in which case, that leaves me out.

On Economics

I've discovered that for people like me, supply and demand don't exist as separate concepts. There's just a constant supply of demands.

On Science

I think it was physicist Werner Heisenberg who came up with the famous Principle of Uncertainty. Yeah. I'm sure of it.

On Music

I once was part of a college ensemble selected to play a piece by modernist composer Earle Brown, who was visiting campus on a lecture tour. My job was to lean over an open Steinway and randomly pluck piano strings, but during the concert a pen accidentally fell out of my shirt pocket and bounced around between the F-sharp and the G. It was later acknowledged as a stroke of genius that had turned an otherwise jejune performance into a musical tour de force.

On Drugs

No. At least I don't think so.

Imagine That

A 22-year-old London girl is selling her imaginary friend on eBay. "My psychiatrist recommended that I say goodbye to Bernard, and although I would like some financial compensation, it is more important that he finds a good home." The seller hopes to get as much as £200 for the best friend.

— Metro.co.uk

Yes. Quite comfortable, thank you. Do you mind if I take off my shoes? I'm sorry, what? There are professional guidelines about clients remaining completely clothed? But it's just my shoes. It was a long walk from the train station, and I... No. No. I get it. That's fine. (awkward silence) Boy. I'd love to know the details behind that little regulation. You want to talk about it? Oh, right. No, no. You don't have to remind me. I'm the patient. You're the doctor. Yes... I'm entirely clear about that.

Well, as best as I can remember, it started my senior year in high school, when I had to invent a prom date. His name was Horst, and while he had impeccable taste in formal wear, he couldn't dance worth a damn. I mean, really. Who does the Lindy Hop to the *Star-Spangled Banner*? I ditched him at McDonalds® when he tried to get to second base in the drive-thru.

Things progressed to another level during my twenties, when I made up an imaginary doubles tennis partner whom I introduced to everybody as Rafael Nadal. For some reason, tournament officials appeared suspicious when our names came up on the contestant list, so I quickly renamed him Horst. Huh? Oh. Yeah. I can see how it might be confusing, but no. This was a completely different guy. A real gentleman. Never laid a hand on me. Although he did have a habit of patting me on the backside with his racquet whenever we scored a point. No. It really didn't go anywhere. Purely competitive, I guess. After we won the runner-up trophy I never saw him again.

Then came my husband Sebastiano, a Basque Spaniard I concocted to take advantage of the less expensive family medical plan offered by the company where I worked. I have to say... he was really well-liked by my friends and co-workers, despite the chronic health issues that kept him from ever showing up at office parties and social gatherings. There was just something about him, you know?

For me, one of his best traits was a free $100,000 spousal life insurance policy that came with the company benefits package. What? Oh, my God, yes. It absolutely broke my heart when he disappeared on that spelunking trip in the Pyrenees, but... hey. What are you gonna do. Besides, there's nothing like drying your tears on a warm Caribbean island, right? Which one? Well, I think it was Eleuthera, but I can't be sure. Wherever it was, I'm pretty certain there was a casino involved.

So, um... where do we go from here? Huh? Oh, my. Well, no. I guess I haven't given it any serious thought. Really? You want me to stop making up imaginary friends and start dealing with reality? Geez, I... That could be kind of difficult, you know? I mean, I'm pretty popular with these guys. I can't imagine what they'd do without me. Oh, right. That's not exactly the point, is it.

Well... OK. I suppose I can give it a try. Is there some prescribed methodology or something? I mean, what's the best way to go about it? I don't want to sound mercenary or anything, but if it's gonna be costly, I may have to put it off. Things are a little tight right now.

You're kidding. eBay? Wow. You really think there's a market out there? Hmm. Yes, of course. I absolutely should be practical. Start small and just list my most recent friend. All right, then. You've convinced me. By God, I'll do it! I'm stoked!

Just one more question.

How much do you think I can get for you?

ASCENDING ORDER

More than 13,000 people in the United States paid a plastic surgeon to enhance their butts last year (2014), according to a new report just released by the American Society of Plastic Surgeons. There were 11,505 buttock augmentation procedures, up 15 percent from 2013.

— Cosmopolitan Magazine

So, um... have a seat. No, not there. Try this OSHA-approved rocker, guaranteed to withstand 3Gs of hyper-gluteal gravitational force.

Good. Now that we're snuggly nestled into the adipose comfort of our oversized derrieres, let me begin by saying "Well played, Cosmo." Once again I find myself embarrassingly (ahem) behind the times. The *Times*, by the way, appears to be embarrassingly behind you, since I recall reading nothing in the New York press that comes close to the topic at hand.

Not that my normally reserved hand would be anywhere near the topic, mind you. But given Newton's law of universal gravitation, which states rather insistently that two bodies will attract each other with a force directly proportional to the product of their asses – sorry, masses – under the right circumstances my relatively puny paw might have about as much choice as a space rock trying to quietly sneak past Jupiter. If it inadvertently happens to lock into orbit around anyone's moon base, please accept my sincerest apologies.

Whence, do you reckon, all the trending toward bloated backsides? I mean, for as long as I can remember, the thrust has generally been in the opposite direction. Not that I have any personal stake, mind you. At this point in my life, most dorsal regions sit well with me. I just wonder why the sudden shift. Call it a cultural curiosity, if you will – an objective, scientific interest in getting to the bottom of things.

I suppose some folks might agree with *Cosmopolitan's* conclusion that it's a celebrity thing, referencing as evidence a

photo of Kim Kardashian's shiny hindquarters that made the – this is almost too easy – rounds earlier this year. But I think it's a weightier issue. I think something profoundly sinister is holding sway here. Something ominous. Something that's just beginning to cast a dark shadow.

Once again, I'm afraid, the answer lies in the seamy and clandestine machinations of the international fashion industry – the same rogues that gave us eyeball-searingly plaid golf slacks and the scourge of spaghetti-thin, nine-inch heels designed to singlehandedly cause a spike in women's hip replacements. Yes, my friends, it all traces, thread by thread, back to a worldwide consortium of criminal clothiers.

Come on. Who else stands to gain so immensely from the flagrant over-exposure of bounteous backsides? Besides a bunch of women intent on eating themselves into the trend, I mean. Fashion designers and fabric manufacturers, that's who.

Think about it. The bigger the butts, the more the bolts of cloth required to cover them. Why scrape by with 20 percent margin on the cost of a size-10 pair of Capri pants if, with a little prodding from the PR side of the operation, you can get 50 percent on XXL? When it comes to the bottom line, there's no place to go but up.

But I suspect there may be something even more going on here. Besides extra inches of adipose tissue. Go ahead. Ask yourself: "Why now? Why such an emphatic focus on inflated back-ends at this particular moment in history?" Could it have anything at all to do with the inevitable and unavoidable effect of gravity on baby-boomer backsides? Is it possible that now would be the perfect time, market-wise, to reposition 20 million well-developed derrieres as the next big thing?

I think we all know the answer to that. And I, for one, intend to rise up against such a crass and obvious exploitation of an entire generation.

Just as soon as the UPS guy arrives with the tire irons I'll be needing to pry myself from this chair.

A GOOD TONGUE-LASHING

Scientists at New York University have determined that it takes approximately 2,500 licks to get to the center of a Tootsie Roll Pop.

– Time

OK. Not necessarily Nobel Prize material, but given the ever-growing number of Twitter tweeters intent on telling the world what they're doing with every tick of the clock – as well as the purely analog need to calculate whether you can squeeze in the required number of licks before it's your turn to visit the confessional – potentially useful information nonetheless. A cocktail party ice-breaker at the very least. ("What a marvelous facility you have with your tongue. I could never reach an ice cube that far down in the glass. Say, here's a little known fact...")

It does make you curious, though, doesn't it, about what led the research team to land on that particular topic. I mean, when you've got a definitive cure for hiccups still out there waiting to be found, why zero in on the deleterious effects of dragging your tongue across a lollipop?

And was it an absolute requirement that the study be undertaken by a bunch of people with advanced degrees? Seems like two kids under a shade tree with some time on their hands might have sufficed. In fact, I was thinking how easy it would be to challenge the results with some experiments of my own. I'd need a control group, though. Let's see. I wonder if the neighbor's dog likes lemon-lime?

Disappointingly, he doesn't. He just likes cherry, and I'll be damned if I'm going to let a bulb-eyed Chihuahua lap his way through the entirety of my private stash – even if it is in the name of science. Anyway, the oddity of the NYU topic selection process has led me to engage in a separate, more wide-ranging study, the results of which I have placed before a review board at the prestigious International Institute of Fewtrils and Useless Tidbits. The subject matter, of course, is fewtrils and useless tidbits. (I don't know. It just seemed somehow appropriate to throw in that last bit of unnecessary information.) Following are a random selection of findings from that report, tentatively titled "Trifles: They're Not Just Chocolate Anymore."

- It takes 22 chews to fully masticate a standard, breakfast-size sausage link. Unless you're from the Ozarks. Then it could take all day.

- On average, it takes about 19 minutes of non-stop snoring before a bed-sharing spouse begins to think about homicide. It's important to note that our analysis specifically discounts a recently televised Fox docudrama about Francine "The Pillow" DeFranco, who apparently just had it in for her husband.

- On Wednesdays, in the precise time slot between 2:17 and 3:03 p.m., 57 percent of all middle-aged American males have less than 79 cents in change in their front-right pants pockets. Inexplicably, they also share that space with at least one individually wrapped Halls Mentho-Lyptus dating back to 1993 or earlier.

- It turns out that socks aren't always for the feet. They also make good puppets. Interestingly, one study participant utilized them for both purposes at the same time, although no one actually got to see the show because it all took place inside his shoes.

- Relatedly, it takes approximately 13 seconds to pull on a freshly washed pair of athletic socks... but only if the wearer isn't engaged in some kind of a matinee performance.

- The term "baker's dozen" is a purely American phrase, and is used by Japanese educators as evidence of an inherent weakness in the U.S. math curriculum.

- For the past five and a half minutes you have been unwittingly involved in a survey whose purpose was to confirm that, on a daily basis, large numbers of usually rational adults are willing to spend an inordinate amount of time dealing with trifles. Five and a half minutes, to be exact...

ABOUT THE AUTHOR

Doug Miller is a writer of long-form fiction, short stories and humorous essays. Other works by the author include the novel *Girl Scouts*; *Secret Shorts*, a collection of humorous short stories and essays; and *Jack Pipe, Plumber and Personal Counselor*, absurdly funny guidance from a fictitious plumber who doubles as a newspaper advice columnist. Yes. You read that right.

All the author's works are available at **booksbymiller.com**